Prayers
to Share

Year C

Dedication

This book is dedicated to the church members and friends who,
through all the Sundays of the church year, have shared prayers with me.
We have offered prayers to God at

Ipswich Road United Reformed Church, Norwich, England
Lakenham United Reformed Church, Norwich, England
Princes Street United Reformed Church, Norwich, England
Knox United Church (Pruden Street), Thunder Bay, Canada
First Church United, Thunder Bay, Canada
St. Andrew's United Church, Schreiber, Canada
Terrace Bay Community Church, Terrace Bay, Canada
Westminster United Church, Thunder Bay, Canada
Duff United Church, Duff, Canada
Grace United, Lemberg, Canada
Knox United, Abernethy, Canada
St. Andrew's, Balcarres, Canada

David Sparks

PRAYERS TO SHARE YEAR C

Responsive Prayers
for each Sunday of
the Church Year

Revised Common Lectionary based

WOOD LAKE BOOKS

Editors: James Taylor and Mike Schwartzentruber
Cover design and layout: Margaret Kyle
Proofreading: Dianne Greenslade

Wood Lake Books Inc. acknowledges the financial support of the Government of Canada,
through the Book Publishing Industry Development Program (BPIDP) for
our publishing activities.
At Wood Lake Books we practice what we publish, guided by a concern for fairness, justice, and
equal opportunity in all of our relationships with employees and customers.
We recycle and reuse and encourage readers to do the same. Resources are printed on
recycled paper and more environmentally friendly groundwood papers (newsprint), whenever
possible. The trees used are replaced through donations to the Scoutrees for Canada program.
A percentage of all profit is donated to charitable organizations.

National Library of Canada Cataloguing in Publication Data
Sparks, David, 1938-
Prayers to share, year C: responsive prayers for each Sunday of the church year/David Sparks.
"Revised Common lectionary based" – t.p.
ISBN 1-55145-489-0
1. Common lectionary (1992). Year C. 2. Pastoral prayers. 3. Church year – Prayer-books
and devotions – English. I. Title.
BV250.S63 2003   264'.13   C2003-910956-9

Published by
Wood Lake Books Inc.
9025 Jim Bailey Rd, Kelowna, BC V4V 1R2
www.joinhands.com

Printing 10 9 8 7 6 5 4 3 2 1

Printed in Canada by
Transcontinental Printing

Contents

WE CAN HELP YOU, YOU CAN HELP US!

This is the second volume of a planned three-volume series. The publisher and the author are encouraged by the enthusiastic reception of *Prayers to Share Year B,* which is being used weekly by worship leaders worldwide.

There have been questions about the need to get permission to reproduce prayers. Put simply, you can reproduce prayers from these books in any church service bulletin or worship aid. If you wish to include them in a book or other document for publication, we need to know about it!

If you have comments, changes, or improvements for the *Year C* book we would like to hear about them. Would a CD or diskettes with all the three volumes be useful to you? We would also be interested to know of your hopes for companion volumes which could help in the weekly preparation of worship. Please send your comments to Michael Schwartzentruber. By mail at:

Wood Lake Books Inc.,

9025 Jim Bailey Road, Kelowna, BC, Canada, V4V 1R2

Or by e-mail to:

mikes@woodlake.com

Preface

To pray, to give thanks and praise to God, who has given us everything and without whom we are nothing, is the most natural act in the world. To be able to pray with other members of the faith community Sunday by Sunday is an awesome privilege.

But what form should this public prayer take?

This is the second of what are intended to be three volumes of *Prayers to Share.* I continue to believe that prayer in worship is not just a solo act of the minister, priest, or lay worship leader. Nor is it an unthinking chorus of leader and people together. It is, or should be, a dynamic, responsive act that captures the hearts and minds of congregational members and brings glory to God.

The *Revised Common Lectionary* provides a solid, scriptural basis for our prayers. Through the lectionary, the seasons of the church year are followed and the wide spectrum of the scriptures, Hebrew and Christian, is honored. Many of the prayers in this book derive from or are inspired by the readings appointed for a particular week or season.

It is my hope that those of you who lead worship will be helped in different ways by the weekly set of prayers provided here. Some of you will find that my style fits well with your own style, and that you can use these prayers as they are printed. Some of you will want to change words or phrases, so that you feel comfortable with them and so that the congregation can sense that the prayers are in tune with their joys, hopes, fears, and with the situation of their faith community. And, no doubt, some of you will simply want to look at the prayer patterns and work out your own themes and words for a particular week: for example, in the "Confession" prayers, I have tended not to use the traditional "miserable offender" approach but to offer affirmations, reminders, encouragement, and questions instead.

For years, the sermon has been considered by many to be the center of the worship experience. In my experience, it is certainly the thing most often commented on by people as they leave the worship service. I believe, however, that a worship service should be a thematic whole and that the prayers, hymns, sermon, music, and dramatic presentation should complement, reflect, and build on one another. Moreover, it is "liturgy" (the work of the people) that we are about. Worship leaders are responding faithfully when the congregation is engaged in worship, and what better way of engaging the congregation than through active, responsive participation in prayers throughout the service?

As I complete this task, I am acutely aware of the ways in which the members of the pastoral charges I have served have fed my prayer life. It is their joy, their challenges, their questions, their tough places, and their reflections on scripture that are mirrored in these pages. To them, and to the One All-Loving God, I offer my profound thanks.

Advent 1

(For Advent in 2003, 2006, 2009, 2012...)

Jeremiah 33:14–16
Psalm 25:1–10
1 Thessalonians 3:9–13
Luke 21:25–36

Call to Worship *(Jeremiah 33:14-16)*

One: The circle of poverty will be broken.
All: Thanks be to God!
One: The vice grip of evil will be shattered.
All: Thanks be to God!
One: The ache of loneliness will be ended.
All: Thanks be to God!
One: The insight of a child will lead us.
All: Thanks be to God!

Or

Call to Worship

One: God's promise will be fulfilled!
All: God's promise will be fulfilled, as the faith community gather, for prayer and thanksgiving.
One: God's promise will be fulfilled!
All: God's promise will be fulfilled, as the suffering are comforted and the poor are empowered.
One: God's promise will be fulfilled!
All: God's promise will be fulfilled, when justice is a priority, and prophets are recognized.
One: God's promise will be fulfilled!
All: God's promise will be fulfilled as the coming of Jesus is embraced, and his Way followed.

Opening Prayer

One: Be alert! God's Promised One is on the way.

All: Be ready with your praise;
be ready to give Jesus a rousing welcome.

One: Be alert! God's Promised One is on the way.

All: Be ready with your friendship;
be ready to make Jesus feel at home.

One: Be alert! God's Promised One is on the way.

All: Be ready to work with others;
be ready to discover Jesus in the faith community.

One: Be alert! God's Promised One is on the way.

All: Be ready to see Jesus in your neighbor,
and to promote God's justice for our troubled world.

One: Be alert!

All: We are an Advent people! Amen.

Prayer of Confession

One: You give the gift of hope, O God.

All: In the pattern of faithful life which brings us pain,
we need your hope.

One: You are the inspirer of hope, O God.

All: In the striving of our faith community to serve this neighborhood,
we need your hope.

One: You are the pattern of hope, O God.

All: In those times when apathy or despair bring us low,
we need your hope.

One: You are the source of hope, O God.

All: In those situations when we struggle to forgive,
we need your hope.

(Time for silent reflection)

Words of Assurance

One: Hope makes the breakthrough,

All: **As new paths are explored,**
and as new opportunities are grasped.

One: Hope makes the breakthrough,

All: **As old rivalries are put aside,**
and as fresh visions are grasped.

One: In the hopeful freedom of the Spirit, you are renewed people.

All: **Pardon and peace are ours. Thanks be to God! Amen.**

Offering Prayer

One: A baby will soon be born;

All: **We will dedicate our best gifts to him.**

One: A child will influence our faith community for good.

All: **His coming will test the generosity of our fellowship.**

One: God's Chosen One will shake our tested routines.

All: **Our response to Jesus will shape how our resources are used.**
Amen.

Or

Offering Prayer

One: What we offer to you, O God, this morning,
gifts of money, talent, and time, can make a surprising difference.

All: **Our money enables skilled persons to go to work**
on our behalf, to bring compassionate help
and a sense of what is just;

One: Our talents, used in your service, bring joy to us the givers,
and a sense of Christ's reality to those who receive;

All: **Our time, given generously,**
enables the life and work of this faith community to thrive,
and the coming of Jesus to be proclaimed,
gloriously and with determination. Amen.

Commissioning

One: Proclaim the coming of Christ!

All: We believe wholeheartedly that evil will be crushed.

One: Act justly and with compassion.

All: We will, even if it costs us dear.

One: Give with generosity of all your diverse gifts.

All: We will work hopefully with the disheartened and depressed.

One: Look beyond your present horizons to a yet more glorious shore.

All: God is with us, in time and beyond time.

Or

Commissioning

One: Look to the Child of Advent!

All: Advent summons us with the exuberant hopefulness of a child.
Advent holds us spellbound with childlike wonder.
Advent challenges us,
for God was made known in a tiny child in a far-off land.

Advent 2

Malachi 3:1–4
Luke 1:68–79
Philippians 1:3–11
Luke 3:1–6

Call to Worship

One: Christmas is coming! Christ, the Promised One, is near!
All: **We will prepare for God's Holy One**
with worship which is warm and joyful.
One: Christmas is coming! Christ, long hoped for, is near!
All: **We will prepare for God's Cherished One**
with friendship which includes the outsiders.
One: Christmas is coming! Christ, the Peace-bringer, is near!
All: **We will prepare for God's Anointed One**
with forgiveness and reconciliation.
One: Christmas is coming! Christ, beloved, is near!
All: **We will prepare for God's Chosen One**
with compassion and sharing.

Opening Prayer

prayer approved Dec 10/06

One: We come before you, Living God,
as travelers on the Advent journey.
As we worship you this morning,
All: **Give us a song in our hearts;**
give us the Word which will sustain;
give us the encouragement of fellow travelers;
give us the sign of peace which Advent brings;
give us the will to make peace.
One: For we pray in the name of Jesus, the Coming One,
whose Way leads to lasting peace:
All: **Peace in our homes,**
peace within the faith community,
peace in our troubled world,
and peace deep within our hearts. Amen.

Prayer of Confession

One: God has provided a long-promised Savior for us.

All: **Salvation comes as we face new realities,**
and leave what's past in the past.

One: God has sustained a sacred covenant with the people of God.

All: **We give thanks for God's gracious goodness,**
but we are aware that we have responsibilities
for worship and for service.

One: God sent John to prepare for the coming of God's Chosen One.

All: **We wonder about the quality of our preparation for the coming of**
Jesus.

One: The dawn of God's light in Jesus, will break gloriously into the world's darkness;

All: **We reflect on the darkness**
that has infiltrated our relationships,
and the life of our faith community.
(Time for silent reflection)

Words of Assurance

One: You guide our steps into the way of peace, O God.

All: **Peace comes, as we take the time to think quietly**
about the paths we have taken;
the paths of forgiveness and justice seeking,
the paths of self-interest and self-serving.

One: Peace comes as we are prepared to leave the routine of the past, to risk and venture as Jesus did.

Offering Prayer

One: God's peace shines through our gifts:

All: **The peace of challenges faced,**
the peace of suffering ones befriended,
the peace of hurts and slights forgiven,
the peace which the Good News proclaims,
the peace of neighborhood justice worked out,
the peace which global justice enshrines,

One: the peace which Jesus embraced.

All: **You will bless our gifts with peace,**
as they are used, O God. Amen.

Commissioning

One: Are you ready for the challenge of Advent?

All: **We will hear the words of the messenger who calls on us to repent.**

One: Are you ready for the challenge of Advent?

All: **We will join with Joseph and Mary on a faithful but difficult journey.**

One: Are you ready for the challenge of Advent?

All: **We will prepare our hearts and minds for God's Chosen One, who is on the way.**

One: Are you ready for the challenge of Advent?

All: **With you beside us, Loving God, we have nothing to fear!**

Advent 3

Zephaniah 3:14–20
Isaiah 12:2–6
Philippians 4:4–7
Luke 3:7–18

Call to Worship

One: God's messenger is coming to prepare the way.

All: We rejoice that God loves us enough to send him.

One: God's messenger has some challenging words to bring us.

All: We are ready to listen and to reflect.

One: God's messenger will call us to action.

All: We will work to make the necessary changes.

Or

Call to Worship

One: John, wild prophet, baptizer,

All: We approach you with fear and anxiety.

One: John, voice of conscience, baptizer,

All: We hear you and are humbled.

One: John, caller to repentance, baptizer,

All: We stand ready to make a fresh start.

One: John, forerunner of Jesus, baptizer,

All: We will seek justice and peace within the community of the baptized.

Opening Prayer

One: We will not find you, Loving God, in the busy stores,
  or among the Christmas lights.

All: But where a young couple struggles to get basic housing, you are there.

One: We will not find you, Caring God, in the packed casino,
  or on the Internet.

All: **But where a refugee seeks a safe place for her family,**
you are there.

One: We will not find you, Compassionate God,
at the bank machine or in a high class restaurant.

All: **But where a newly bereaved person searches**
for a comforting presence, you are there.

One: Ever-present God, we will follow you,

All: **Faithfully, calmly, as we proceed on our Advent journey. Amen.**

Prayer of Confession

One: Do you hear the challenge of John the Baptist?
Sharing is in style!

All: **In John's day, food and clothes;**
Today? Tax breaks for the poor,
low cost housing, and aid for developing nations.

One: Do you hear the challenge of John the Baptist?
Don't abuse power!

All: **In John's day, cheating tax collectors;**
Today? Unfeeling government officials,
and our selfish control of other persons.

One: Do you hear the challenge of John the Baptist?
Don't accuse anyone falsely!

All: **In John's day, bullying soldiers;**
Today? Those who spread rumors,
and tarnish the reputation of others.

One: Do you hear the challenge of John the Baptist?
Take Jesus seriously!

All: **In John's day, the Chosen One of God;**
Today? The same Jesus, whose acceptance tests us,
whose Cross-death challenges us.

(Time for silent reflection)

Words of Assurance

One: The words of John the Baptist come home to us.

All: We will reflect carefully, and repent practically!

One: You will experience God's pardon and peace.

All: And we will thank our Gracious God. Amen.

Or

Prayer of Confession

One: From the wilderness,

All: The Baptist cries "Repent!"

One: The food banks are busier than ever, the welfare rolls grow,
the strain of the holiday season begins to show.
From the wilderness,

All: The Baptist cries "Repent!"

One: Pressure grows for standards of health care to be lowered,
the needs of those who have suffered loss are not understood,
the anxious fail to find someone who will listen.
From the wilderness,

All: The Baptist cries "Repent!"

One: Children feel excluded from adult decisions,
seniors struggle to get the services they need,
single parents get no relief from keeping the strain of home and work
in balance.
From the wilderness,

All: The Baptist cries "Repent!"

One: We find it hard to give time to our faith community,
we hold back from caring
for those outside the family and friendship circle,
we recognize our reluctance to respond
to the demands for a just society, a just community,
with our time and resources.
From the wilderness,

All: The Baptist cries "Repent!"
(Time for silent reflection)

Words of Assurance

One: The austere prophet John has called us to repent,
and we have heard his voice.

All: **We will make clear our repentance
in changed attitudes, priorities, and lifestyles.**

One: We have heard John's voice.

All: **We will make clear our repentance
in renewed vision and faithfulness.**

One: God grants you pardon and peace.

All: **Thanks be to God. Amen.**

Or

Words of Assurance

One: You have heard the challenge of John,
you have been called to repent.

All: **We will reflect carefully,
we will weigh our options diligently,
and we will go forward in the Way,
and in the strength of Jesus Christ.**

One: Pardon and peace will assuredly be yours!

All: **Thanks be to God! Amen.**

Offering Prayer

One: O God, sometimes the choices you offer are hard choices:

All: **To share rather than to take for ourselves,
to befriend rather than to ignore,
to tell the truth rather than evade,
to stay faithful, rather than stay with the crowd.**

One: Then you face us with John the Baptist, and his challenge to repent,
and you face us with Jesus, and his Way of love,
and the right choice is clear.

All: **May these offerings enable us to make the faithful choices,
which bring glory to you, O God,
and bring closer your Realm of peace and mutual respect. Amen.**

Or

Offering Prayer

All: May these offerings, gladly given, enable the church
       to support women and men, boys and girls,
       in making choices which will bring glory to you,
       and bring closer your Realm of peace and compassion. Amen.

Commissioning

One: Time for a change!

All: **We will speak out when we find injustice!**

One: Time for a change!

All: **We will work carefully to nurture community!**

One: Time for a change!

All: **We will face loss with gentleness, and reality!**

One: Time for a change!

All: **We will forgive the deepest hurts gradually!**

One: Time for a change!

All: **We will prepare for the coming of Christ thoroughly!**

Advent 4

Micah 5:2–5a
Luke 1:47–55 or Psalm 80:1–7
Hebrews 10:5–10
Luke 1:39–45, (46–55)

Call to Worship *(adapted from the Magnificat)*

One: Like Mary, we praise God wholeheartedly,
from the depths of our souls.

All: For God has not forgotten us, insignificant as we feel ourselves to be.

One: God's name is Holy; God's compassion lasts from one generation to another.

All: God has scattered the proud, and shown that kings and rulers are nothing special.

One: God has lifted up the lowly, and given food to the hungry.

All: God has kept the promises made to the people of God; God will always be merciful. Thanks be to God!

Opening Prayer

One: God of Grace, come close to us and bless us.
As Mary was surprised by the visit of the angel,

All: Prepare us for the Holy, the unexpected, at this season.

One: As Mary carefully thought out the meaning of the angel's visit,

All: Enable us to reflect on the meaning of Christ's coming for us.

One: As Mary courageously allowed God's way to become her way,

All: Show us how we can work in faith together.

One: As Mary voiced God's care for the poorest and humblest of all people,

**All: Give us courage to stand beside those
who have least in the world.
Come close to us and bless us,
as you blessed Mary with Jesus.**

A Christmas Prayer of Confession

One: Mary was blessed in the angelic announcement of the coming of Jesus.

All: **Blessed with questioning, blessed with acceptance,**
blessed with joy at God's precious gift,
blessed with a sense of justice.

One: Mary was blessed in caring for the baby Jesus.

All: **Blessed with surprise, blessed with endurance,**
blessed with a good partner in fearful times,
blessed with memories.

One: But later on, Mary was disturbed by the lifestyle of Jesus,
kept away when she wanted to come close to her son.

All: **Disturbed by his new vocation,**
disturbed by his popularity,
disturbed by his distancing from family.

> *(Time for silent reflection)*

Words of Assurance

One: We too are blessed through the coming of Jesus.

All: **Blessed with joy, blessed with fresh insight,**
blessed with his spirit of compassion,
blessed with his burning zeal for justice.

One: Yet, like Mary, we have been challenged by aspects of his life.

All: **Challenged by his level of commitment,**
challenged by his empathy,
challenged by his acceptance.

One: God enables each one of us to see our life, and its goals,
more clearly through the life of Jesus.

All: **The old ways are at an end!**
Peace, and a new way of life, is ours for the asking.
Thanks be to God. Amen.

Offering Prayer

One: For the supreme gift of Jesus, we thank you, Living God.

All: **As bells ring out,**
as joy breaks out,
as light shines out,
we recognize the blessing these gifts will bring,
and we rejoice! Amen.

Doxology *(tune: Old 100th)*

All: **God's love is come at Christmas time,**
God's love in Jesus brightly shines,
God's Spirit love is on the move,
Our gifts are blessed and shared in love.

Commissioning

One: As we leave this sanctuary, we leave in the spirit of Mary.

All: **We have the blessing of God, for us and with us.**
We give thanks that God has chosen us to serve.
We have confidence that God will give power to the poor,
and put the influential in their place.
In our joy, and in our troubles,
we know that God will be our Savior,
today, tomorrow, and when time turns into eternity.

One: Go with your loving God, for God's love goes with you.

All: **Thanks be to God!**

Christmas Eve/Day

Christmas, Proper 1 (Years A, B, C)

Isaiah 9:2–7
Psalm 96
Titus 2:11–14
Luke 2:1–14, (15–20)

Call to Worship

One: Come good friends, come to Bethlehem!

All: Come to Bethlehem, and celebrate a newborn child with Mary and Joseph.

Women and Girls: Come to Bethlehem, and rejoice that God's symbol of love is a tiny, helpless baby.

Men and Boys: Come to Bethlehem, and sing praises with the shepherds for what God has done.

One: Come to Bethlehem, and fall silent in awe and wonder.

(Time for silent reflection)

One: Jesus is born. God's Word lives!

All: Praise be to God. Alleluia! Alleluia! Amen.

Prayer of Christmas Thanksgiving

One: Thank you, Loving God, for Christmas.

All: Thank you for gifts and for decorations.
Thank you for family, friends, and visitors.
Thank you for good food and drink.
Thank you for the opportunity to give to *(insert names of church mission groups, local charities, special Christmas appeals, as appropriate).*

One: Thank you for Jesus Christ.

All: His teachings were so practical,
his acceptance of the poor and vulnerable so willing,
his opposition to evil so total,
his relationship with God so firm.

One: Thank you for Jesus Christ,

All: **Who is with us this day! Amen.**

Or *sing "Happy Birthday" to Jesus. (Because the words and music are copyright, they are not printed in this book.)*

Lighting of the Christ Candle

One: Bright burns the candle,

All: **Its light ends darkness for each person.**

One: Bright burns the candle,

All: **Clear symbol of Jesus, light of all the world.**

One: Bright burns the candle,

All: **Warm presence; friendships and family close.**

One: Bright burns the candle,

All: **The faith community enlightened through fellowship.**

One: Bright burns the candle,

All: **A sign of hope for the dying, the prisoner, and the despairing. Glorious light, holy light!**

Prayer of Confession at Christmas

One: We enjoy the good things of Christmas so much;
the brightly wrapped gifts, the turkey, the decorated tree.

All: **Yet we know there will be empty plates,**
and homes where there are no gifts, this holiday season.

One: We enjoy the special people of Christmas so much;
family members home for the holidays, good friends,
and those from whom we receive cards and letters.

All: **Yet we know there will be people lonely at this time of company,**
and those who feel the ache of loss.

One: We enjoy the worship of Christmas so much;
the candle lighting, the gospel "Birth of Jesus" stories,
the wonder of "The Word made flesh."

All: **Yet we know it will be hard to sustain our faithful response**
to Jesus Christ throughout the year.
(Time for silent reflection)

Words of Assurance

One: The birth of Jesus, your Beloved, O God,
gives us confidence that we can make changes for good.

All: **It will be possible to bring food to the hungry,
friendship to the lonely, and faith to the searching.**

One: The birth of Jesus affirms the joy of new beginnings!

All: **Thanks be to God! Amen.**

Offering Prayer

One: Joyfully we sing praises to God's Precious One.

All: **Joyfully we hear the Christmas story,
and find Jesus, come to stay.**

One: Joyfully we present our gifts for the work of Jesus today.

All: **We give thanks to God, source of all joy. Amen.**

Or

Doxology *(tune: Old 100th)*

All: **God's love has come at Christmastime.
God's love in Jesus brightly shines.
God's Spirit love is on the move,
Our gifts are blessed and shared in love.**

Commissioning

One: Christ is born!

All: **God's gentle power defeats powerlessness.**

One: Christ is born!

All: **God's loving power enfolds our fearfulness.**

One: Christ is born!

All: **God's presence is known and felt
and celebrated amongst us.**

One: Christ is born!

All: **God's Word comes home,
and sends us out to serve with compassion.**

Christmas Eve/Day

Christmas, Proper II (Years A, B, C)

Isaiah 62:6–12
Psalm 97
Titus 3:4–7
Luke 2:(1–7), 8–20

Call to Worship

One: A father to be, feeling the weight of responsibility, far from home, anxious;

All: **Joseph, God is with you!**

One: A mother to be, wondering about childbirth, far from her family, troubled;

All: **Mary, God is with you!**

One: *(For Christmas Eve)* A child in the womb, warm, secure, waiting;
(or, for Christmas Day) A child snug in his mother's arms;

All: **Jesus, God is with you!**

One: The love of God, surrounding the holy family,

All: **And surrounding our families always.**

Opening Prayer

One: Mary's child, born in poverty, born far from home;

All: **We come to worship Jesus, isolated from his wider family, vulnerable as a newborn.**

One: Mary's child, a source of wonder, a source of inspiration;

All: **We come to worship Jesus, gracefully given, a source of grace to the powerless and dispirited.**

One: Mary's child, a threat to the powerful, a threat to the religious;

All: **We come to worship Jesus, hope to the oppressed, fresh inspiration to the questioning.**

One: Mary's child, objective of the despised shepherds, and of the star-seekers;

All: **We come to worship Jesus, baby most adored, with a future both world- and life-changing.**

Prayer of Affirmation

One: God's love will prevail in spite of loneliness;

All: **Within the holy family, far from support,
far from friends, God's love was found.**

One: God's love will prevail, in spite of loss;

All: **Within the holy family, deprived of shelter
at a crucial time, God's love was found.**

One: God's love will prevail in spite of fear;

All: **Within the holy family, threatened by Herod,
God's love was found.**

One: God's love will prevail in spite of despair;

All: **Within the holy family, forced to become refugees in Egypt, God's
love was found.**

    (Time for silent reflection)

Words of Assurance

One: Nothing can separate us from the love of God, as we have experienced
it in Jesus Christ.

All: **It was there for us in the past,
it is with us right now,
it will be up ahead of us in the future.**

One: A love without exceptions, a love without boundaries, a love whose
power cannot be broken.

All: **Thanks be to you, O God, ever present, ever loving. Amen.**

Offering Prayer

One: We offer our gifts for blessing, O God.

All: **We offer our gifts, O God, as the angels offered praise;**
we offer our time, O God, as the shepherds offered an amazing
witness;
we offer our talent, O God, as the Magi faithfully and fearlessly
offered gold, frankincense, and myrrh.
The offerings on that first Christmas are a blessing to us today.

One: We know you will bless our offerings for the present-day work of Jesus
Christ. Amen.

Commissioning

One: Look to the Holy Child, and encourage all who nurture children.

All: **We look to the Holy Family, and promote love within the family**
circle.

One: Look to the Incarnate One, and see the Divine shine through the
ordinary.

All: **We look to God's Anointed, and prepare a place for him in our**
hearts.

One: Look to God's Precious One, and see the beloved who was not afraid
to venture out.

All: **We look to the Chosen One of God, who will go with us on our**
life's journey.

First Sunday after Christmas Day

(New Year)

1 Samuel 2:18–20, 26
Psalm 148
Colossians 3:12–17
Luke 2:41–52

Call to Worship

One: This is the place,

All: **The place where God is joyfully worshipped.**

One: This is the time,

All: **The time we know that God is with us in the coming year.**

One: These are the friends,

All: **The friends who celebrate with us and stay with us when the testing comes.**

One: This is the faith,

All: **The faith in Jesus Christ, which challenges us and shapes our future.**

Or

Call to Worship

One: The joy of a carver with a new block of wood.

All: **The excitement of a reader with a new book.**

One: The response of a musician to a new tune.

All: **The love of a mother for a new baby.**

One: The sense of adventure in a new path taken.

All: **For all our new starts, we give God thanks.**

One: Let us worship God!

Opening Prayer

One: This is the time for new beginnings.

All: **This is the time for reflection.**

One: This is the time for taking stock.

All: **This is the time for setting faithful New Year goals.**

One: This is the time for putting old grudges and resentments to rest.

All: **This is the time for seeking new friends and fresh avenues of Christian service.**

One: This is the time for renewing our faith in Jesus Christ.

All: **This is the time to rejoice in Christ's presence amongst us. Amen.**

Or

Opening Prayer

One: The old year has gone;

All: **The new year is here, with the promise of worship.**

One: The old year has gone;

All: **The new year is here, with the promise of new truth.**

One: The old year has gone;

All: **The new year is here, with the promise of friendship.**

One: The old year has gone;

All: **The new year is here, with the promise of an end to injustice.**

One: The old year has gone;

All: **The new year is here, with the assurance that you, our loving God, are eternally with us. Amen.**

A New Year's Prayer of Confession

One: We celebrate our joys and achievements in the past year, O God.

All: **We reflect on the hardship, the unexpected change, the setbacks – all the situations from which we may learn and grow.**

One: We celebrate our friendships and family ties, O God.

All: **We reflect on the times of uncaring, poor communication, and of relationships strained –**
all the situations from which we may learn and grow.

One: We celebrate the fulfillment we have found within the faith community.

All: **We reflect on missed opportunities for worship and service, and on our blindness to the work of the wider church –**
all the situations from which we may learn and grow.

One: We celebrate the discipleship of Jesus Christ which is ours.

All: We reflect on our struggle to hear the call of Jesus, to follow Jesus carefully, and to take his Word to heart –
all the situations from which we may learn and grow, in faith and action.

(Time for silent reflection)

Words of Assurance

One: A new year, a new set of resolutions, O God!

All: **Resolved to give thanks regularly,**
resolved to reflect diligently,
resolved to make changes appropriately,
resolved to act faithfully.

One: Pardon and peace are yours.

All: **Thanks be to God! Amen.**

Offering Prayer

One: Enable us, O God, to leave behind token support for this church, and for Jesus Christ.

All: **We resolve to serve you in the New Year,**
joyfully, generously, and wholeheartedly. Amen.

Commissioning

One: We leave this church,

All: **Resolved to face the situations which test and trouble us,**
resolved to take courage from the stories of our faith,
resolved to be a willing partner in the faith community,
resolved to go forward confidently,
resolved to model our New Year's way on Jesus Christ.

One: You have nothing to fear!

Epiphany

Isaiah 60:1–6
Psalm 72:1–7, 10–14
Ephesians 3:1–12
Matthew 2:1–12

Call to Worship

One: A star shining brightly in the East,

All: **Discovered, by those who have eyes to see the unusual and the challenging.**

One: A journey into unknown territory,

All: **Taken by those who have courage and curiosity.**

One: An encounter with an evil, commanding presence,

All: **Evil that was faced, yet resisted with care.**

One: The Holy One recognized, in spite of humble origin,

All: **The glory and the gifts, given to God's Chosen Child.**
Let us worship God!

Opening Prayer

One: We recognize your Epiphany gifts, O God.
As one of the Magi brought frankincense,

All: **So we bring our wholehearted worship to you,**
and ask that you will bless our praise and prayer.

One: As one of the Magi brought myrrh,

All: **So we bring our recognition of Jesus your Anointed One,**
whose life and death is salvation for us and our world.

One: As one of the Magi brought gold,

All: **So we affirm our joyful loyalty to Jesus,**
who brings your glorious Realm closer.
Bless every gift that we bring to Jesus Christ, O God,
and enable us to use these gifts in compassionate service. Amen.

Prayer of Confession

One: Living God, your star in the East guided the Magi to Jesus your
Chosen Child, but it was a disturbing and difficult journey.

**All: When we lack the courage to venture into unfamiliar territory,
O God, forgive us.**

One: Your star led the Magi to grapple with Herod, an evil person.

**All: When we fail to name a source of evil,
or fail to affirm the good, O God, forgive us.**

One: Your star came to rest over the birthplace of Jesus Christ, where gifts
were given him.

**All: When we fail to bring our best gifts, or our most appropriate gifts,
to serve you, O God, forgive us.**

One: Your star was left behind as the Holy Family fled the anger of Herod to
Egypt.

**All: When we are not able to see the refugee,
or to help the stranger in our neighborhood,
O God, forgive us.**

(Time for silent reflection)

Words of Assurance

One: You care about the gifts that are ours, O God, and you want us to
recognize them, and to use them well.

**All: You will bless us when we confront our lack of courage,
and decide to take the rough but right way.**

One: God will go with you when you do!

All: And we will rejoice in God's supportive presence.

One: Pardon and peace are yours!

All: Thanks be to God! Amen.

Prayer of Confession for Epiphany

One: We bring you our gifts, Loving God;
we have no gold, but we offer you our money.

**All: Enable us to share wisely
the gifts you have entrusted to us.**

One: We bring you our gifts, Loving God;
we have no frankincense, but we offer you our worship.

One: Bless our offerings, O God!

All: Enable us to praise joyfully, to pray wholeheartedly,
and to learn with openness from your Word.

One: We bring you our gifts, Loving God;
we have no myrrh, but we offer you our experience of loss.

All: Enable us to express our feelings openly,
to share our struggles trustingly, and to comfort sensitively.
(Time for silent reflection)

Words of Assurance

One: God, glorious Giver, who has given us Jesus the perfect gift,

All: Accept all the gifts we offer, and enable us to give
in the compassionate and generous spirit of Jesus.

One: Where we have withheld our gifts, free us.

All: Where we have been grudging in our giving, open us to generosity.
Amen.

Offering Prayer

One: Bless our offerings, O God!

All: In offering, we will receive your gift of challenge;
in offering, we will receive your gift of compassion;
in offering, we will receive your gift of gratitude;
in offering, we will receive your gift of peace.

One: We offer our gifts in the name of Jesus Christ,

All: whose self-offering completes ours. Amen.

Commissioning

One: Follow the star!

All: We will search for, and find, the highest good.

One: Follow the star!

All: We will recognize the forces of darkness,
and work against them.

One: Follow the star!

All: We will be ready to acknowledge our gifts and use them.

One: Follow the star!

All: We will find fulfillment within the family of Jesus,
and take his Good News to our corner of the world.

1st Sunday after the Epiphany

(Baptism of the Lord)

Isaiah 43:1–7
Psalm 29
Acts 8:14–17
Luke 3:15–17, 21–22

Call to Worship

One: Sign of wonder,

All: God's love graced to humanity in Jesus.

One: Sign of celebration,

**All: The joy of Jesus, alive in persons
who have nothing of their own.**

One: Sign of community,

**All: Christians together, baptizing, sharing communion,
learning and worshipping, giving and serving.**

One: Sign of the times,

**All: Getting and spending does not satisfy,
but the Way of Jesus leads to the true life.**

Opening Prayer

One: Creator God, God of the falling snow,
God of the awesome Northern Lights,

All: We praise you!

One: Creator God; God of the smiling, searching baby,
God of all our years,

All: We thank you!

One: Creator God; God of the Word,
God of inspiring Hebrew and Christian scripture,

All: We listen to you!

One: Creator God; God of inspiration and example to humanity in Jesus,

All: We respond to you, in time and beyond time. Amen.

Or

Prayer of Thanksgiving

One: Joyfully we thank you for this our faith community,

**All: For its life of worship, its links of fellowship,
its work of challenge and compassion.**

One: Joyfully we thank you for the sacrament of baptism,

**All: For its sign of new birth, its sign of welcoming friendship,
its promise of discipleship.**

One: Joyfully we thank you for your Beloved One, Jesus,

**All: For his moment of anointing, his will to mission,
his unswerving purpose.**

One: We rejoice that we may be counted among the company of the
baptized.

**All: May we be worthy of the One
whose baptism tests our faith journey
and secures us within the family of God. Amen.**

A Prayer of Choices (Confession)

One: We remember the willingness of Jesus to choose a life of courage,
compassion, faithfulness, and concern for the downtrodden.

**All: We reflect on the life's choices we have made,
and the choices which lie ahead of us.**
(Time for silent reflection)

One: We remember the willingness of Jesus to choose a committed life with
a community of disciples, very different in viewpoint, background, and
ability.

**All: We reflect on the choices we have made within our family and our
faith community, for good or ill,
and the choices which lie ahead of us.**
(Time for silent reflection)

One: We remember the willingness of Jesus to confront the corrupt prac-
tices, the stagnant traditions, and the evil powers of his time.

**All: We reflect on the choices we have made for justice and right, and
the choices which lie ahead of us.**
(Time for silent reflection)

Words of Assurance

One: You give us the courage, O God,
　　　to choose life in all its fullness.

All: **To choose service rather than apathy,**
　　　freedom rather than dependence,
　　　fellowship rather than going it alone.
　　　As the faithful way comes home to us,
　　　so the need for pardon and peace is strong within us.

One: In the name of Jesus Christ,
　　　receive God's pardon, know God's peace.

All: **Thanks be to God! Amen.**

Offering Prayer

One: Joined as brothers and sisters in Christ,
　　　we have received God's gifts beyond measure.

All: **Joined as builders, as those who shape the faith community,**
　　　we offer our gifts
　　　and ask for God's blessing.

One: Joined in the discipleship of Jesus,
　　　we offer gifts for the distressed, the suffering,
　　　those who lack opportunity, and those who lack confidence,
　　　and ask for God's blessing.

All: **Joined as those who have been richly blessed,**
　　　we are confident that we too can be a blessing. Amen.

Commissioning

One: Remember the common ties which are yours in baptism.

All: **We remember the strength which is ours as members of the church.**

One: Consider the crying needs which are around you.

All: **We remember the determination which is ours to meet those needs.**

One: Remember the faithful community of the baptized who have gone
　　　before you.

All: **We remember the continuous inspiration of Jesus Christ, his words**
　　　in the gospels, and the deeds of his saints.

2nd Sunday after the Epiphany

Isaiah 62:1–5
Psalm 36:5–10
1 Corinthians 12:1–11
John 2:1–11

Call to Worship

One: Sign of wonder at a wedding…

All: The gifts of Jesus go joyfully to work.

One: Sign of celebration at a wedding…

**All: Jesus brings all that is necessary
to those whose resources have failed.**

One: Sign of commitment at a wedding…

**All: Jesus displays his best talents
with a compassionate and generous act.**

One: Sign of God's glory at a wedding…

**All: The influence of Jesus for good is seen and recognized.
It will be recognized in our church and in our community.**

Prayer of Thanksgiving

One: We thank you, O God, that we can join together as members of the
faith community,

**All: Celebrating the presence of persons from so many different back-
grounds in the family of Jesus Christ.**

One: We thank you, O God, that we can join with Christians of all the ages,

**All: Celebrating the trusted tradition of prayer, praise, and joyful
worship.**

One: We thank you, O God, that we can join with those who study the
Word,

**All: Celebrating the inspiration of scripture, alert for the prophetic
message, and challenged by the Way of Jesus Christ.**

One: We thank you, O God, that we can join with those who put faith into
practice,

All: Celebrating the influence of Christian values,
       at home, at school, in the workplace,
       and wherever poverty and powerlessness are confronted. Amen.

A Prayer of Confession

One: Loving God, you are closer than the breath that is within us,
       you know us better than our best friend,
       you care for us more deeply than our closest family member,
       you desire us to be utterly faithful; and so

All: When confidence deserts us,
       when energy for good leaves us,
       when compassion abandons us,
       when zest for forgiveness and justice cannot be found within us,
       you call us to reflection, confession, and new resolution.
          (Time for silent reflection)

Words of Assurance

One: All seeing, all knowing, all understanding God,

All: You challenge us, you enlighten us,
       you call us to new ways.

One: The life which lies ahead for you will be joyful;
       God's peace will be at the heart of it.

All: Thanks be to God. Amen.

Offering Prayer

One: These gifts, O God, are signs of our faithfulness to you.
       Bless them.

All: Bless them as the faith community comes alive in worship;
       (If appropriate) Bless them as our community is enriched through
       baptism/confirmation.
       Bless them as your Word comes home to us, and renews us;
       Bless them as the compassion of Jesus Christ goes to work through
       us. Amen.

Commissioning – Epiphany

One: You have signed us with the cross, O God;
      may we be signs of Jesus Christ!

**All: A sign of community to the lonely,
      a sign of hope to the discouraged,
      a sign of compassion to the downhearted,
      a sign of challenge to the apathetic,
      a sign of love to the rejected.**

One: In the spirit of Christ we have everything to gain!

3rd Sunday after the Epiphany

Nehemiah 8:1–3, 5–6, 8–10
Psalm 19
1 Corinthians 12:12–31a
Luke 4:14–21

Call to Worship

One: Look for the signs of God's presence.
All: **There is celebration in the air, joy abounds!**
One: Look for the signs of God's presence.
All: **The lonely are noticed, community grows!**
One: Look for the signs of God's presence.
All: **The oppressed are freed!**
One: Look for the signs of God's presence.
All: **Those who cannot understand receive insight!**
One: Look for the signs of God's presence.
All: **The suffering find compassion, the bereaved find comfort!**
One: Look for the signs of God's presence.
All: **God's Word is taken to heart. Faith is alive!**

Opening Prayer

One: You call us together,
All: **As a Christian community.**
One: You inspire us to prayer and praise,
All: **As brothers and sisters in the faith.**
One: You challenge us to listen and learn,
All: **As searchers for the truth.**
One: You invite us to support each other,
All: **As compassionate friends.**
One: You confront us,
All: **With the injustice of our neighborhood and nation.**
One: You send us out,
All: **To show the face of Christ to a hurting world. Amen.**

A Prayer for Community

One: When we are in community, Loving God,

All: **We will be aware of the joys and frustrations of those around us.**
(Time for silent reflection)

One: When we are in community, Loving God,

All: **We will be aware of the gifts and talents of community members, and encourage their use.**
(Time for silent reflection)

One: When we are in community, Loving God,

All: **We will plan and work to bring Good News to our neighborhood.**
(Time for silent reflection)

One: When we are in community, Loving God,

All: **We will take the love of Christ to heart, and show the love of Christ to the downhearted, the oppressed, the bewildered, and those who feel trapped.**
(Time for silent reflection)

Words of Assurance

One: This is our belief,

All: **In our growing sense of oneness in Christ, in our willingness to know and root out our selfishness, we will find the salvation we seek,**

One: The salvation which Christ lived and died.

All: **Amen.**

Or

Prayer of Confession

One: We drink from the cup of plenty;
      we have so many of this world's good things!

All: **You call us to strive for simplicity,**
      and to actively support the poor.

One: We drink from the bitter cup;
      we have experienced loss and grief.

All: **You call us to express our feelings,**
      and to grasp the extended hand of friendship.

One: We are able to drink freely;
      the powerful ones do not intimidate us.

All: **You call us to stand with the oppressed,**
      to work to free the imprisoned,
      and with those enslaved by fear and tradition.

One: We drink hopefully from the cup,
      for God's Realm will be established!

All: **You call us to speak and act,**
      so that the evil ones will be overcome,
      and the Way of Christ prevail.

One: We drink from the communion cup,
      yet we neglect our common participation
      in the work of the faith community.

All: **You call us to examine the Christian life we share,**
      and resolve to work joyfully and constructively with others.
        (Time for silent reflection)

Assurance of Pardon

One: Out of your generosity, O God, you enable us to confess openly and
      honestly.

All: **You steer us towards new attitudes and new directions, but the**
      action is up to us!

One: Give us the resolve and the courage, not just to confess our faults, but
      to bring change,

All: **For we know, O God, that when we do,**
      your pardon will be received,
      and our peace will be your peace. Amen.

Offering Prayer

One: We offer to you, O God,

All: **Our gifts, for your blessing;**
our talents, committed for Jesus;
our community, strengthened for service. Amen.

Commissioning

One: As we leave this church, break down the barriers that divide us:

All: **The barrier of superiority that keeps us from seeing the ability of others;**

One: The barrier of pride that keeps us from accepting new ways and new truth;

All: **The barrier of apathy, that keeps us from acting justly, and mercifully;**

One: The barrier of indifference, that keeps us from giving and experiencing the love of God;

All: **The barrier of superficiality, that keeps us from revealing our true selves.**

4th Sunday after the Epiphany

Jeremiah 1:4–10
Psalm 71:1–6
1 Corinthians 13:1–13
Luke 4:21–30

Call to Worship

One: Gathered as a worshipping community,

All: We respond to God with prayer and praise.

One: Gathered as a learning community,

All: We respond to God by listening for God's Word.

One: Gathered as a compassionate community,

All: We respond to God with acts of caring.

One: Gathered as a serving community,

All: We respond to God as we identify the powerless and stand beside them.

Opening Prayer

One: Living God, in the turmoil of our world,

**All: We come before you,
searching for calm and understanding.**

One: In the uncertainty of our faith community,

**All: We come before you,
searching for a confident way with Jesus.**

One: In the ups and downs of family life,

All: We come before you, searching for joy together.

One: In the time of individual challenge,

All: We come before you, searching for faithful resolution. Amen.

Prayer of Confession

One: We thank you, O God, for the call to be your faithful people,

All: But we confess we have not listened carefully to your Word.

One: We thank you, O God, for the call to be your compassionate people,

All: But we confess we have ignored the signs of suffering.

One: We thank you, O God, for the call to be your committed people,

All: But we confess our commitment has been to a comfortable way.

One: We thank you, O God, for the call to be people of justice,

All: But we confess we have been unwilling to listen to, and act for, the oppressed.

(Time for silent reflection)

Words of Assurance

All: In listening with our heart, in responding with a will,
in looking to the person of Jesus Christ,
the way ahead will be clear to us,
and peace will abide in us.

One: Feel God's pardon: for you, with you, before you.

All: Thanks be to God! Amen.

Offering Prayer

One: As we offer gifts, we will receive the awareness of giving with others for common goals.

All: As we offer gifts, we will receive the awareness
that deep needs can now be met –
within this faith community,
within communities of this nation,
and beyond these shores.

One: As we offer gifts, we will know your blessing with us, the givers, O most loving and generous God. Amen.

Commissioning

One: You are called from your very different situations, as servants of the one loving God.

All: We are called to serve with fellow Christians within this lively faith community.

One: You are called to serve in the Way of Christ beyond the boundaries of this church.

All: We are called to serve the downtrodden and confused,
the lonely, sad, and misunderstood,
the ones Christ served.

5th Sunday after the Epiphany

Isaiah 6:1–8, (9–13)
Psalm 138
1 Corinthians 15:1–11
Luke 5:1–11

Call to Worship

One: A vision for our faith community, a vision of joyful worship.

All: **Voices praising, young and old together, God's name glorified.**

One: A vision of faithfulness to God's Word.

All: **The challenge of the prophets, heard;**
the psalms, a strength;
the teachings of Jesus, the Way to follow.

One: A vision of compassionate service.

All: **The powerless empowered, the weak supported, the vulnerable**
given self-confidence.

One: A vision with the love of Jesus Christ at the center.

All: **Let us worship God!**

Or

Call to Worship

One: As the disciples encountering Jesus were acutely aware of their priorities,

All: **So we come before you, God,**
ready to look at life differently.

One: As the disciples were ready to tell their family and friends about Jesus,

All: **So we come before you, God,**
refusing to keep our faith to ourselves.

One: As the disciples faithfully trusted and found their trust wonderfully
rewarded,

All: **So we come before you, God,**
prepared to put our loyalty to the Christian way
before all else.

One: As the disciples found that responding to Jesus' call was the most
challenging event of their life,

All: **So we come before you, God,**
and hear the words of Jesus, "Follow me!"

Prayer of Approach

One: You are with us as we encourage each other to risk new paths, O God.

All: **In the challenging times, your love is gracefully given and received.**

One: You confront us with unforeseen opportunities, fresh avenues of
service.

All: **In the midst of self-doubt, and when we question our own motives,**
you secure us, O God.

One: You challenge us with a call to faithful discipleship, O God.

All: **In the use of our best gifts and talents, your Realm comes closer.**

One: You identify with the troubled and distressed, O God.

All: **As we are aware of the lowly and serve the needy, we are caring for**
Christ.

One: You are the Good News for our times, O God:

All: **A note of hope amid the despair,**
a sense of truth when it seems that nothing can be trusted. Amen.

Prayer for Our Faith Community (Confession)

One: The community of faith welcomes newcomers and makes them feel at
home.

All: **Where our welcome is half-hearted or superficial,**
O God, forgive us.

One: The community of faith is sensitive to the youngest,
sustains in times of hectic parenthood,
and is there in the challenging later years.

All: **Where our care is unfeeling, or ignores the vulnerable,**
O God, forgive us.

One: The community of faith searches out the talents of members old and
new.

All: **Where we refuse to try out new skills, where we ignore offers to**
help or to take responsibility, O God, forgive us.

One: The community of faith looks beyond its own fellowship to the wider church, and to the downtrodden of other nations.

All: Where our service is short-sighted, and our giving limited to the needs of our own fellowship, O God, forgive us.

One: The community of faith is not afraid to disclose new truth about the gospel, or listen to today's prophets.

All: Where we cling to well-worn ways of interpreting scripture, and close our ears to new words of justice, mercy, and peace, O God, forgive us.

(Time for silent reflection)

Words of Assurance

One: You are at the heart of our faith community, O God.

All: You will open our eyes to realities we would rather avoid.

One: You will enable us to hear the words we would rather not hear.

All: You will give us the strength to follow the path which leads to new and untried ways.

One: Pardon and peace do not come without struggle and reflection, but God will grant you a new heart and a new start.

All: Thanks be to God! Amen.

Offering Prayer

One: It is in our offering, O God, that we show our Christian commitment,

**All: And we are committed –
committed to sustaining the work of the local church,
committed to building up ministry in this neighborhood,
committed to serving the wider church in our mission gifts,
committed to caring for those whose names we don't know, but whose needs we recognize,
committed to making clear that the Christian faith brings life.**

One: Bless these gifts, O God, and put us to work with them. Amen.

Or

Offering Prayer

One: These gifts faithfully proclaim our commitment.

All: **They provide companionship to the lonely,
comfort to the sick, justice to the oppressed,
and hope to those who have suffered loss.
Bless them as token of all we can give and be, in Christ. Amen.**

Commissioning

One: Go from here to fulfill your calling as disciples of the Way of Jesus.

All: **We will listen for God's Word,
we will live with abundant hope,
we will promote justice,
we will be compassionate,
we will seek out new friends,
we will strengthen the faith community.**

One: And the grace of Jesus Christ,
who teaches, saves and sustains,
will go with you.

All: **Amen.**

6th Sunday after the Epiphany

(If this is the Sunday before Ash Wednesday, this Proper may be replaced by the readings for the last Sunday after Epiphany, Transfiguration Sunday.)

Jeremiah 17:5–10
Psalm 1
1 Corinthians 15:12–20
Luke 6:17–26

Call to Worship

One: We come before you, our source and our sustainer.

All: Praise be to you, O God. You hold us and the world in your hands.

One: We worship you, our hope throughout the years and generations.

All: Praise be to you, O God. You are eternally to be trusted.

One: We adore you, O God. Your Way is revealed by the prophets and made clear in Jesus.

All: Praise be to you, O God. Your justice never fails, your compassion goes beyond our understanding.

Opening Prayer

One: O God, great Creator,

**All: Show us how to thank you
for the sustaining power of your creation.**

One: O God, great Teacher,

All: Give us the insight and grace to respond to your challenging Word.

One: O God, compassionate One,

All: Enable us to sense your caring presence in the testing times and to feel secure.

One: O God, eternal Hope,

All: Grant us the wisdom to believe that your love is for us in life, and beyond life. Amen.

Prayer of Resolution

One: In the struggles of everyday living, you are with us, O God.
In the support of family members,

All: You give us patience.

One: In the hard places of decision making,

All: You give us the will to weigh up alternatives carefully.

One: When conflicts come between friends or at work,

All: You give us the desire to reconcile,
and the will to make a fresh start.

One: In the times of ill health or personal setback,

All: You give us the courage to endure,
and the strength to go forward hopefully.

One: When we have suffered loss,

All: You give us a clear vision,
a vision of life which will be good once more.
(Time for silent reflection)

Words of Assurance

One: When our confidence falters, you are there, O God!

All: You will not let us give up, or stay disheartened,
or be walked over, or put down.

One: You affirm our worth in your sight, and stand by us,
as you stood by Jesus.

All: And we rejoice in a new sense of self-esteem!
Thanks be to you, O God! Amen.

Or

Words of Assurance

One: In careful reflection you address us, O God.

All: In a resolve to change our ways, you encourage us, O God.

One: As we set out again to live faithfully, O God,

All: You grant us pardon and peace. Amen.

Offering Prayer

One: These gifts will root us in the faith community, O God.

All: **They enthuse us to bring change in the name of Jesus Christ;**
they inspire us to share the compassionate Christian spirit;
they send us out to work faithfully for Christ;
they remind us that we are responsible for sustaining many beyond
our fellowship;
Bless them, O God. Amen.

Commissioning

One: You assure us that no adversary, no adversity,
will defeat us, O God.

All: **You inspire us to live our dreams.**

One: You have given the life and the cross-death
of Jesus Christ to free us.

All: **You send us out to prove our discipleship.**

One: In our faithfulness, you bless us!

All: **As we serve, you work with us.**

7th Sunday after the Epiphany

(If this is the Sunday before Ash Wednesday, this Proper may be replaced by the readings for the last Sunday after Epiphany, Transfiguration Sunday.)

Genesis 45:3–11, 15
Psalm 37:1–11, 39–40
1 Corinthians 15:35–38, 42–50
Luke 6:27–38

Call to Worship

One: Trust in God!

All: Our trust is well founded.

One: Trust in God and give thanks to the Gracious One!

All: Our thanks is wholehearted, and full of joy.

One: Trust in God in the company of the faithful!

All: Our friends in Christ support and nurture us.

One: Trust in God and serve God generously!

All: Our aim is to reach the powerless, and work with justice.

One: Trust in God!

All: Our trust is well founded.

Opening Prayer

One: God does amazing things for us.

All: God is revealed as Creator and encourages us to create.

One: God surprises us all the time.

**All: God is revealed in the downtrodden and suffering,
and calls us to respond.**

One: God inspires us day by day.

**All: God is revealed when hope is found,
and temptations are overcome.**

One: God has come to us in Jesus Christ.

**All: Jesus is revealed as the evil ones are confronted,
and the faithful way is taken. Amen.**

Prayer of Confession *(based on Luke 6:27–38)*

One: "Love your enemies!"

All: **Loving God, we will try, but it is so hard to understand and forgive.**

One: "Do good to those who hate you."

All: **Loving God, we will try, but they will not come halfway to meet us.**

One: "Bless those who curse you."

All: **Loving God, we will try, but our temptation is to curse them back.**

One: "If anyone strikes you on the cheek, offer the other."

All: **Loving God, we will try, but it is so natural to return violence with violence.**

> *(Time for silent reflection)*

Assurance of Pardon

One: Loving God, you give us the strength to take the right
but difficult course of action.

All: **You encourage us to forgive;
you are with us when we go the extra mile;
you restrain us when we seek revenge;
you remind us to walk away from violence.**

One: You will find peace, when you face your enemies in the Spirit of God.

All: **We will. Thanks be to God! Amen.**

Offering Prayer

One: Gifts without limit we have received from you, O God,
and we return our gifts, joyfully and with thankfulness!

All: **We give, so that the Way of Jesus may be known
through the life of our faith community:**

One: A way of encouragement and support,

All: **A way of compassion and practical help,**

One: A way of concern for the needy of this suffering world,

All: **A way of concern for the needy in this neighborhood,**

One: A way that we are called to walk together,

All: **A way that Christ has shown clearly to us. Amen.**

Commissioning

One: Go from here as God's empowered people!

All: **We are ready to forgive.**

We will hear the pain of those around us.

We will stay with those who have suffered loss.

We will be intolerant of the unjust.

We will draw attention to the evil ones.

We will challenge the patronizing.

We will strive after humility.

We will follow the saints of Christ.

One: And God will smile on you!

Last Sunday after the Epiphany

(Transfiguration Sunday)

Exodus 34:29–35
Psalm 99
2 Corinthians 3:12 – 4:2
Luke 9:28–36, (37–43)

Call to Worship

One: Known in the Law of Moses,

All: God, we greet you!

One: Your justice made known by the prophets,

All: God, we welcome you!

One: Your love made clear by Jesus,

All: God, we adore you!

One: Your way followed by martyrs and saints,

All: God, we worship you!

One: You are with us and for us today,

All: God, we thank you!

Opening Prayer

One: The light of Christ will enlighten our worship.

All: The joy of Christ will echo in our praise.

One: The light of Christ will enlighten our worship.

All: The friendship of Christ will bind us together in community.

One: The light of Christ will enlighten our worship.

All: The acceptance of Christ will mark our relationships.

One: The light of Christ will enlighten our worship.

All: The faithful commitment of Christ will shine through our service. Amen.

Prayer of Confession

One: O God, give us grace to lift up our eyes from the routine and everyday,

All: **To grasp a vision of your awesome creative majesty.**

One: O God, give us grace to stand back from the familiar friendships and family ties,

All: **To see the worth of each person in your sight.**

One: O God, give us grace to lift up our eyes from "the way things have always been,"

All: **To see them transformed by your radiant presence.**

One: O God, give us grace to carefully consider our priorities,

All: **And measure them against the priorities of wholeness and compassion highlighted for us by Jesus Christ.**

(Time for silent reflection)

Words of Assurance

One: The view from the mountaintop is awe inspiring,
but you cannot remain there.

All: **In our careful reflection and our deliberate confession,
we come down to earth.**

One: You are ready for new opportunities, new ventures,
and fresh responsibilities. Pardon and peace are yours.

All: **Thanks be to God! Amen.**

Offering Prayer

One: These gifts will enable the faith community
to see others in a fresh light.

All: **To see newcomers as friends in the making,
to see the old-timers, and discover fresh gifts, new talents,
to see the suffering as persons we can stand beside,
to see children as those from whom we can learn,
to see our neighborhood through God's just eyes,
to see our world and know we can make a difference.**

One: With a renewed vision there are no limits to what may be achieved.

All: **Thanks be to God! Amen.**

Commissioning

One: You will be transformed!

All: **Transformed by our response to Jesus Christ,
transformed by the gracious love of God,
transformed by partnership with the Holy Spirit.**

One: You *will* be transformed!

Ash Wednesday

Joel 2:1–2, 12–17 or Isaiah 58:1–12
Psalm 5:1–17
2 Corinthians 5:20b – 6:10
Matthew 6:1–6, 16–21

Call to Worship *(based on Joel 2:12–17)*

One: "Repent and return to God," says the prophet.

All: We know that confession and repentance will be our focus.

One: "God is gracious and merciful," says the prophet.

All: As our faults come home to us, we need God's mercy.

One: "God is slow to anger, and abounding in steadfast love," says the prophet.

All: The abiding love of God gives us hope.

One: "Gather the people, assemble the aged, gather the children," says the prophet.

**All: We come as a faithful people before you, O God.
We are ready for the Lenten time of reflection.**

Opening Prayer

One: To come into your presence, O God, is a humbling experience.

All: We come aware of our faults, ready to be renewed.

One: To come into your presence, O God, is a learning experience.

All: We come aware of our ignorance, eager to receive new truth.

One: To come into your presence, God, is a challenging experience.

**All: We come aware of the crying needs of our city and world,
ready to serve the downtrodden, and the exploited.**

One: To come into your presence, O God, is the experience of a lifetime.

**All: We come aware of your eternal goodness,
ready to witness to your glorious presence in Jesus Christ.
Amen.**

Prayer of Confession

One: When we see ourselves as superior,
   when we insist on our own way,

All: Mark us with the ashes of repentance, O God.

One: When we will not claim our abilities, when we defer to others,

All: Mark us with the ashes of repentance, O God.

One: When we deny the value of faith community,
   when we see faith as personal experience,

All: Mark us with the ashes of repentance, O God.

One: When we practice a local Christianity,
   when we cannot see need beyond the horizon,

All: Mark us with the ashes of repentance, O God.

One: When we feel our beliefs are sufficient,
   when we are not open to new truth,

All: Mark us with the ashes of repentance, O God.

One: When we accept the compassionate way of Jesus,
   but will not take the hard sacrificial way,

All: Mark us with the ashes of repentance, O God.
   (Time for silent reflection)

Words of Assurance

One: You humble us, O God,
   but you will not leave us without hope.

**All: You call us to repent, but you will not desert us
   as we make a fresh beginning.**

One: God who loved you in the beginning, loves you still.
   Be assured that God stays with you, in all the twists and turns of life.

All: We know God's peace; nothing can overturn it!

One: Nothing!

All: Thanks be to God. Amen.

Offering Prayer

One: You will not leave us in the dust, O God.

All: You will raise us up!

One: And with these gifts, you will raise the desolate and downhearted:

All: The lonely will find a friend,
the sinner will know forgiveness,
the rejected will be affirmed,
the suffering will find hope,
the bereaved will experience comfort,
the searcher will come to faith.

One: These gifts are powerful.

All: They are, thanks be to God! Amen.

Commissioning

One: Pray quietly, God is listening.

All: We will confess openly, for God is forgiving.

One: Pray from the heart, God encourages you.

All: We will hold nothing back, for God is with us.

One: Pray in community, God binds you together.

All: We will pray for each other, and we will be strengthened.

One: Pray in the spirit of Jesus, his love goes with you.

All: We will pray confidently, and root his love in action.

Lent 1

Deuteronomy 26:1–11
Psalm 91:1–2, 9–16
Romans 10:8b–13
Luke 4:1–13

Call to Worship

One: Lead us, O God, as we enter the Lenten season.

All: **Give us the courage of Jesus,**
who did not hang back from confronting evil.

One: Lead us, O God, as we enter the Lenten season.

All: **Give us the dedication of Jesus,**
who was not diverted from preaching the Gospel.

One: Lead us, O God, as we enter the Lenten season.

All: **Give us the compassion of Jesus,**
who saw the suffering ones and was moved to help them.

One: Lead us, O God, as we enter the Lenten season.

All: **Give us the faithfulness of Jesus,**
who saw the cross but did not turn back.

Opening Prayer

One: In moments of reflection,

All: **May we know the peace of your presence, O God.**

One: In the offering of prayer,

All: **May we hear your still small voice, O God.**

One: In the quiet places of our life,

All: **May we be aware of your gentle leading ,O God.**

One: In the sacred church moments,

All: **May we sense your Holy Spirit, O God,**
bringing us together for service in the Way of Jesus. Amen.

Prayer of Confession

One: "Lead us not into temptation."

All: We are tempted to take the easy but flawed path.

One: "Deliver us from evil."

All: Evil flourishes when apathy and selfishness take root in us.

One: "Lead us not into temptation."

All: We are tempted to avoid the needs of family members and those around us.

One: "Deliver us from evil."

All: Deliver us from the evil that is an intimate part of us,
and from the darkness we choose to ignore
in our neighborhood, our society, and our church.
(Time for silent reflection)

Words of Assurance

One: The God who knows us through and through, the God who realizes our potential for good, calls on us to change our flawed ways and meet the needs of others.

All: We are intent on change;
we will no longer tolerate the suffering of others.

One: God promises you pardon and peace!

All: Thanks be to God! Amen.

Offering Prayer

One: The vision of a vulnerable young man refusing to compromise with evil, giving away everything, even his life – the vision of Jesus Christ is before us.

All: In remembrance of his sacrifice we give;
in following his example of acceptance and compassion, we give;
in response to his concern for wholeness, we give;
to work for the good of suffering humanity, we give;
to bring equality to this unjust world, we give.
Bless our offering, O God. Amen.

Commissioning

One: As we go forward into the coming week, we will be tempted with meeting practical needs and forgetting the spiritual.

All: Jesus said, "One does not live on bread alone."

One: We will be tempted to control others and gain personal advantage.

All: Jesus said, "Worship the Lord your God and serve God alone."

One: We will be tempted to get God to change situations which are way beyond our power to change.

All: Jesus said, "Do not put the Lord your God to the test."

One: In every temptation, God will be a present strength. Go in peace!

Lent 2

Genesis 15:1–12, 17–18
Psalm 27
Philippians 3:17– 4:1
Luke 13:31–35 or 9:28–36

Call to Worship

One: Living God, our companion,

All: **We come before you on our Lenten journey.**
We pause. We wait for you.

One: It is a journey which will be taken reflectively.

All: **Our spirits long for the refreshment which God will provide.**

One: It is a journey which will be taken in faith.

All: **Jesus, our teacher and example, has gone ahead of us.**

One: It is a journey which we take as Christians together.

All: **We have so much encouragement to give to each other.**

One: In this act of worship we are equipped for the journey.

All: **Thanks be to you, O most generous and supporting God.**

Opening Prayer

One: The work of Jesus Christ began with his baptism;

All: **Our baptism roots us in the community of faith.**

One: His work continued with teaching which touched people's hearts;

All: **We hear the stories of Jesus and we are moved to action.**

One: The healing and challenging work went on, despite opposition open and subtle;

All: **His refusal to bow down to rulers, religious and political, led to a cross.**

One: It seemed that his work was over, but on the third day, death was defeated;

All: **The rising of Jesus gives us hope and a promise that in our work, we will have a faith companion. Amen.**

Or

Opening Prayer *(in unison)*

All: Come with us into the faith filled community, O God;
   your truth to inspire us,
   your word to instruct us,
   your joy to dance with us,
   your love to enfold us, every step of the way. Amen.

Prayer of Confession

One: Jesus chose to take the lonely, dangerous road to Jerusalem.

All: **We identify our reluctance to take the unknown path.**

One: Jesus was pressured by the disciples to stay out of harm's way.

All: **We identify our temptation to avoid the path of right and justice.**

One: Jesus knew that powerful ones were conspiring to silence him.

All: **We identify our feelings of fear, when we are weak and vulnerable.**

One: Jesus believed that in facing death, God would be with him.

All: **We identify our call to faith, when facing the trials and hard places of life.**

   (Time for silent reflection)

Words of Assurance

One: The God who gives us courage;
   the God who stirs our conscience;
   the God whose justice is a shining light, goes with us.

All: **We will take heart;**
   we will be strong;
   we will change our direction;
   we will travel faithfully,
   knowing that Christ has gone before us,
   faced the cross, and overcome dead ends and death.

One: We have peace in Christ.

All: **Thanks be to God. Amen.**

Offering Prayer

One: Although these are *our* gifts which we bring for blessing, O most
generous God, they were first *your* gifts.

All: **We have received everything from you, O God.**
Joyfully, gracefully, thankfully, we return a small portion for
faithful service.

One: If these gifts bring comfort, if they bring friendship,
if they bring hope, then your Name will be glorified,
and the example of Jesus Christ followed.

All: **Praise be to you, O God! Amen.**

Commissioning

One: Obedient to Jesus, God's Chosen One, we leave this church,

All: **Ready to question commands carefully, and investigate laws**
thoroughly;
ready to confront the powers rigorously;
ready to explore scripture regularly, and grow spiritually;
ready to act faithfully, and endure graciously;
ready to work co-operatively,
to build Christian community.

Lent 3

Isaiah 55:1–9
Psalm 63:1–8
1 Corinthians 10:1–13
Luke 13:1–9

Call to Worship *(Psalm 63:1–5 adapted)*

One: God, you are our God. We long for you.

All: Like a parched, dry land, our souls are thirsty for you.

One: Your constant love is the ground of our being; it is life itself.

All: As long as we have breath, and beyond, we will joyfully praise you.

Opening Prayer

One: A baby stirs in her sleep, a youngster calls out for his mother.

All: And we recall your creative and caring presence, O God.

One: A family party rocks with laughter, and a bereaved family comes together in grief.

All: And we remember your joyful and compassionate presence, O God.

One: A protestor shouts of injustice, and the plight of a political prisoner is made public.

All: And we are aware of your merciful and encouraging presence, O God.

One: The struggle of Jesus is recounted, and his death on a cross looms closer.

All: And we know, that your saving love goes beyond our imagining, O God. Amen.

A Lenten Prayer of Confession

One: A time of decision making for Jesus;
     to keep to the country byways, or take the Jerusalem highway.

All: Be with us in our time of decision making, O God.

One: A time of discouragement for the disciples;
     Jesus choosing to confront the powerful ones.

All: Be with us when we feel powerless and afraid, O God.

One: A time when the rulers, religious and political,
feel threatened by the good and generous Way of Jesus.

All: Be with us when we are tempted to compromise with truth or
compassion, O God.

> *(Time for silent reflection)*

Words of Assurance

One: We are sure of God's response to our deepest concerns.

All: Into our anxiety and fear, O God, you breathe calm.
Into our failure and lack of courage, O God,
you breathe confidence.
Into our doubt and uncertainty, O God, you breathe faith.

One: God's peace will enfold you; God's love will surround you.

All: Thanks be to God. Amen.

Offering Prayer

One: These gifts will provide friendship.

All: These gifts will provide laughter.

One: These gifts will encourage sharing.

All: These gifts will encourage learning.

One: These gifts will be your voice.

All: These gifts will be the words and intentions of Jesus.
Bless these gifts, O God. Amen.

Commissioning

One: Seek out those who are hungry and thirsty, in mind, body, and spirit.
Meet their deepest needs!

All: In our hunger for the authentic life, and in our spiritual thirst,
we will bring our needs confidently to you, our loving God.

Lent 4

Joshua 5:9–12
Psalm 32
2 Corinthians 5:16–21
Luke 15:1–3, 11b–32

Call to Worship

One: God is with us this morning!
All: **Calling us to friendship, calling us to praise.**
One: God is with us this morning!
All: **Calling us to listen, calling us to respond.**
One: God is with us this morning!
All: **Calling us to confess, calling us to forgive.**
One: God is with us this morning!
All: **Calling us to celebrate, calling us to follow Jesus.**

Opening Prayer

One: A love that will not let us go,
All: **You have declared the height, breadth, and depth of your love in Jesus Christ:**
One: A love that searches out the lost and rejected,
All: **A love that brings wholeness and healing,**
One: A love that is not satisfied with half-truths or evasion,
All: **A love that confronts evil and injustice head on,**
One: A love that accepts the despised and unlovely,
All: **A love that stayed faithful to you, O most loving God, all the way to the Cross. Amen.**

Prayer of Confession and Recognition *(based on Luke 15:11–24)*

One: Loving God, we have squandered many of the gifts that you have lavished on us:
All: **Gifts of creation, gifts of friendship, gifts of trust, gifts in family.**
One: Loving God, we have cut ourselves off from your love and security.

All: **We have followed our own self-interest,**
lived for the moment, forgotten our roots.

One: But, Loving God, we have realized our own failures, we have turned for our faithful home.

All: **We are amazed that you still embrace us,**
dumbfounded that you will forgive us.

One: Loving God, we will join in the family celebration you provide for us,

All: **Rejoicing in your generosity, determined to make a fresh start.**
(Time for silent reflection)

Words of Assurance

One: O God, can your love for us be as accepting, as forgiving, as far reaching, as compassionate, as total, as you lead us to believe?

All: **In the light of your love in the person of Jesus Christ, our doubts**
fall away.

One: We are confident that you, O God, will bring the impact of our shortcomings home to us, and will equip us to begin again.

All: **We will be modern disciples to be reckoned with!**
We will build up the faith community!
We will use our talents generously!

One: You can rely on us, Loving God!

All: **We praise and thank you! Amen.**

Offering Prayer

One: The generosity of your love overwhelms us, O God.

All: **We can simply stand in awe, but you call us to respond, and these**
gifts are a token of our response.

One: We give, so your love may be shared with those who need it so badly, O God:

All: **Peace-bringing love to those in pain of mind or body;**
empathetic love to those who have suffered loss;
tough love to the powerful and oppressive;
practical love to the hungry and the homeless.

One: Remembering your generous love in Jesus, we ask for your blessing. Amen.

Commissioning

One: Respond to the love of God!

All: **We will trust unfailingly,**
we will learn carefully,
we will listen deeply,
we will share generously,
we will resist temptation confidently,
we will repent wholeheartedly,
we will celebrate joyfully,
we will respond to Jesus daily.

One: God will strengthen your resolve,
God's blessing will go with you!

Lent 5

Isaiah 43:16–21
Psalm 126
Philippians 3:4b–14
John 12:1–8

Call to Worship

One: We gain all things in Jesus Christ.
All: **The words of Jesus are there to comfort us in distress.**
One: We gain all things in Jesus Christ.
All: **The deeds of Jesus are there to inspire us to action.**
One: We gain all things in Jesus Christ.
All: **The Cross of Jesus is there to proclaim God's love.**
One: In Jesus Christ,
All: **We gain the good and compassionate Way.**

Opening Prayer

One: The gift of Mary,
All: **The gift of her presence
to a friend facing testing and death.**
One: The gift of Mary,
All: **The gift of her generosity,
to disciples who had still much to learn.**
One: The gift of Mary,
All: **The gift of her commitment
to the teacher who was her inspiration.**
One: The gift of Mary,
All: **The gift of her love to God's Chosen One,
in whom God's love is revealed. Amen.**

Or

Opening Prayer

One: Strengthen us on our Lenten journey, O God.

All: Give us the spirit of determination which Jesus made clear.

One: Affirm us on our Lenten journey, O God.

All: Give us that belief in our talents and abilities which was lived out by Jesus.

One: Call us to reflection on our Lenten journey, O God.

All: Give us the willingness to confront hard choices, as Jesus did.

One: Renew us on our Lenten journey, O God.

All: Give us that faith in your love which held Jesus secure. Amen.

Lenten Prayer of Confession

One: The Cross is ahead for us, as it was for Jesus.

All: When we hang back from venturing into uncharted territory, Lively God, encourage us.

One: The Cross looms menacingly, as it did for Jesus.

All: When our fears threaten to overcome us, Caring God, be our friend.

One: The Cross challenges community values, as in Jesus' time.

All: When we are inclined to go along with the crowd, Just God, challenge us.

One: The Cross symbolizes sacrifice, as it did for Jesus.

All: When we are prepared to compromise our faith, Renewing God, stand with us.

  (Time for silent reflection)

Words of Assurance

One: We are in solidarity with Jesus on the journey to Jerusalem.

All: As we walk the rough walk with him,
as we accept the consequences for faithful decisions,
as we know God's presence with us every step of the way, the peace of God is sure.

One: The pardon of God is yours to gracefully receive.

All: Thanks be to God. Amen.

Offering Prayer

One: Touch our gifts with Mary's generosity of spirit, O God,

All: **That they may touch the sad, the lonely, and the powerless,
in the Way of Jesus. Amen.**

Commissioning

One: Like Mary, give us insight, O God, to understand the stress and the
struggle of our loved ones.

All: **Like Mary, encourage us, O God,
to generously help those who are hard pressed.**

One: Like Jesus, enable us to acknowledge, O God,
the generous spirit of the giver's gift,

All: **And may the aroma of generosity fill the self-seeking and unjust
corners of our troubled world.**

Or

Commissioning (together)

All: **Glorious Creator, we will praise you!
Careful Nurturer, we will thank you!
Compassionate Friend, we will rely on you!
Generous Giver, we will follow your example!
Love without an end, we will accept and share your love!**

Lent 6
Palm/Passion Sunday

(For Liturgy of the Palms)
Luke 19:28–40
Psalm 118:1–2, 19–29

(For Liturgy of the Passion)
Isaiah 50:4–9a
Psalm 31:9–16
Philippians 2:5–11
Luke 22:14–23:56 or Luke 23:1–49

Call to Worship

One: Joyous, enthusiastic!
All: We join the crowds who welcomed Jesus.
One: Supportive, friendly, encouraging!
All: We join the disciples who came with Jesus.
One: Wondering, reflective, in awe!
All: We look towards the cross-hill of the city.

Opening Prayer

One: Touch us with your joy, O God,
All: As we acclaim Jesus, your praiseworthy One.
One: Encourage us with your Word, O God,
All: As we learn from Jesus, your wise and inspired Son.
One: Fill us with your compassion, O God,
All: As we follow the lead of Jesus, your care-full One.
One: Unite us as your people, O God,
**All: *(As Passion Sunday)* As we share bread and wine,
     and remember Jesus, your beloved Son. Amen.**
**All: *(As Palm Sunday)* As we pray and praise together,
     and remember Jesus, your beloved Son. Amen.**

Or

Opening Prayer

One: Jesus Christ, we greet you with enthusiasm!

All: **We join the crowds, we walk with the disciples, we shout,**
"God bless the One who comes in the name of the Lord!"

One: Jesus Christ, we wonder at your courage!

All: **We eat the Passover supper with you;**
we go with you to the suffering place of Gethsemane.

One: Jesus Christ, we are amazed at your endurance!

All: **We sense the hatred of the religious establishment;**
we know the weakness of tyranny.

One: Jesus Christ, we stand in awe of your death!

All: **We stand silent beneath the Cross;**
we cannot believe that you have been killed!

One: Jesus Christ, of palm branch and of nail, you will come through to Easter!

All: **And we know that the agony is not in vain! Amen.**

A Confessional Meditation

One: We see ourselves with the crowds at Jerusalem, easily swayed,

All: **Enthusiastic, welcoming Jesus one moment,**
crying "Crucify him!" soon after.

One: We see ourselves among the disciples at Jerusalem, first supportive and then fearful,

All: **Joyfully acclaiming Jesus as "Messiah" and "Son of David," then**
running away when the pressure is on.

One: We see ourselves with the political and religious leaders of Jerusalem, threatened and exposed,

All: **Knowing in our hearts that he speaks the truth,**
yet afraid of living out that truth.

One: We see ourselves with Jesus at Jerusalem, tempted yet secure,

All: **Aching to run for cover, yet believing that the love and justice of**
God is worthy of sacrifice.

(Time for silent reflection)

Words of Assurance

One: You meet us at the most testing times of life, O God,

All: **Knowing the choices that are ours,**
making clear the cost of the faithful way,
believing that we have the strength to win through, for Christ.

One: Jesus has gone before you. His cross symbolizes the agony, but also the victory. Accept the peace of Christ.

All: **The peace of Christ is ours. Thanks be to God! Amen.**

Offering Prayer

One: Gifts; clothes strewn in his path; a carpet of palm branches; tokens of loyalty, tokens of enthusiasm.

All: **These gifts; tokens of thanksgiving, tokens of commitment,**
instruments of compassion and service.

One: As you blessed your Holy One, O God, bless these gifts now,
for they are given in remembrance of Jesus. Amen.

Or

Offering Prayer

One: The pain, of one falsely accused.

All: **The loss, of one whose friends let him down.**

One: The agony, of one who is suffering cruelly.

All: **Bless these gifts, O God, given to help the crucified;**
in the church, in our troubled world, and within our family circles.
Amen.

Commissioning

One: The joy of Jesus, welcomed into Jerusalem.

All: **We leave this church with joy, O God,**
ready to inspire joy.

One: The pain of Jesus, rejected and abused, crucified.

All: **We leave this church feeling the pain, O God,**
ready to relieve deep hurt.

One: The hope of Jesus, who says, "Into your hands I commit my spirit."

All: **We leave this church with hope, O God,**
ready to create a climate of hope.

Holy Thursday

Exodus 12:1–4, (5–10), 11–14
Psalm 116:1–2, 12–19
1 Corinthians 11:23–26
John 13:1–17, 31b–35

Call to Worship

One: Servants of the Living God, take notice!

All: **Jesus, the Compassionate One, has gone about his work of healing.**

One: Servants of the Living God, listen carefully!

All: **Jesus, the One who accepts, has been on the side of the ignored and despised.**

One: Servants of the Living God, consider the One who serves!

All: **Jesus, the One who serves compassionately, takes a bowl and towel and washes the disciples' feet.**

One: Servants of the Living God, be still and wonder!

All: **Jesus, the Anointed One of God, is willing to go to the Cross rather than compromise his convictions.**

Opening Prayer

One: With bowl and towel, there is compassion.

All: **We ready ourselves to serve those who cry out for acceptance and empowerment.**

One: With bowl and towel, there is humility.

All: **We recognize how much we are served by those who are near and dear to us.**

One: With bowl and towel, there is understanding.

All: **We realize that service is given through the use of many varied gifts.**

One: With bowl and towel, there are broad horizons.

All: **We lift our eyes to see the crying needs of many nations.**

One: With bowl and towel, there is a reminder of Jesus.

All: **We affirm our following of God's Chosen One, whose faithfulness leaves us breathless. Amen.**

Prayer of Confession

One: We remember Peter, who refused to believe Jesus would have to suffer and die.

All: **We remember those times when we cannot see the reality that stares us in the face.**
(Time for silent reflection)

One: We remember Mary, who in an extraordinary act covered the feet of Jesus with expensive ointment.

All: **We remember those times when we have held back from generously giving to others.**
(Time for silent reflection)

One: We remember Jesus, who washed the feet of his friends.

All: **We remember those times when we have missed opportunities to be of service to those around us.**
(Time for silent reflection)

One: We remember Jesus taking the rough road to Jerusalem.

All: **We remember those times when we are called to walk the challenging Way of Christ, even though it may lead to a cross.**
(Time for silent reflection)

Words of Assurance

One: As we remember our failings and shortcomings, we are tempted to say, "What's the use!"

All: **You remind us, O God, that it is not in our perfection that you accept us, but in our willingness to confess our faults and start again.**

One: "A humble and contrite heart, O God, you will not despise."

All: **And so we know that your pardon will be for us, and your peace will be our peace.**

One: It will! In time and beyond time!

All: **Thanks be to God! Amen.**

Offering Prayer

One: Generously you have given gifts to us, Loving God, and you call for a generous response.

All: **Through these gifts of money, you call us to care thoughtfully for those in this congregation we know so well.**

One: Through these gifts of money, you call us to serve persons in this nation, and those beyond its shores, whose names we will never know.

All: **Through the gift of friendship you call us to serve with empathy those challenged and suffering, and to comfort those who have been bereaved.**

One: Through the gift of faith community, you call us to care generously for those who are committed to this church, and those who call on the church in time of need.

All: **Through the gift of faith, you call us to accept pastoral care for ourselves;**
to be willing to admit our fear, or our sense of guilt, to a trusted friend;
to put aside the pride that refuses to admit that help is needed;
to believe without reservation that your love is for us and with us all the time, and will never leave us.
We pray in the name of Jesus, in whom your love was fully known. Amen.

Commissioning

One: People of God, go out to serve.

All: **We will serve faithfully, for the example of Jesus is before us.**
We will serve generously, for the needy are around us.
We will serve patiently, for small, determined steps make up the journey of faith.
We will serve thankfully, for we have been given so much to be thankful for.
We will serve gracefully, and give God the glory.

Good Friday

Isaiah 52:13 – 53:12
Psalm 22
Hebrews 10:16–25 or Hebrews 4:14–16, 5:7–9
John 18:1 – 19:42

Call to Worship

One: Take us to Golgotha, O God;
     show us the maimed figure on the Cross.

All: **Show us a young woman,**
     legs shattered by a land-mine in Cambodia.

One: Take us to Golgotha, O God;
     show us the tortured figure on the Cross.

All: **Show us a young man led into drug addiction in our city.**

One: Take us to Golgotha, O God;
     show us the abused figure on the Cross.

All: **Show us the face of a child,**
     molested by one she knows well.

One: Take us to Golgotha, O God;
     show us the frail figure on the Cross.

All: **Show us the old Jew, scarred by a holocaust of inhumanity.**

One: Take us to Golgotha, O God;
     show us the sorrowful figure on the Cross.

All: **Show us the young Jew whose face**
     is etched with the agony of all humankind.

Opening Prayer

One: The "sacred head sore wounded";

All: **The mind of a wise teacher who teaches us still.**

One: The feet pierced with nails;

All: **A young man, who could "walk the walk" as well as "talk the talk."**

One: The hands battered and bloody;

All: **Hands that reached out to heal,**
     gently bringing calm where there was fear.

One: The side cruelly pierced;

All: **A violent act to one who sought an end to violence.**

One: Jesus on the Cross, mortally wounded;

All: **We give thanks and praise to you, O God,
for the gift of Jesus, your Loved One and our salvation.
Amen.**

Prayer of Separation and Confession

One: The friends of Jesus could not share his distress and his isolation of spirit, in Gethsemane.

All: **We hear a call, to be compassionate to those who are going through times of testing.**

One: Peter, in the High Priest's courtyard, denied any knowledge of Jesus.

All: **We hear a call to speak the truth, especially when it is easier to evade the truth.**

One: The disciples hid away at the time of trial and execution.

All: **We hear a call to resist the powerful and to stand with the powerless.**

One: The cry of Jesus, "My God, my God, why have you forsaken me?"

All: **We hear a call to remember that at the moment we feel God's absence most acutely, God is present.**

   (Time for silent reflection)

Words of Assurance

One: Loving One, Holy One, God of Hope, you will be with us;

All: **Bringing friendships, when we feel alone,
bringing courage, when we feel afraid,
bringing hope, when we feel at a loss,
bringing peace, when we feel troubled.**

One: The peace of God, through which you can confidently begin again.

All: **Thanks be to God. Amen.**

Offering Prayer

One: What can we offer, O God, when we reflect on all you have given us in Jesus Christ?

All: **We will offer our talent, time, and treasure, committed to the One who gave all for us. Amen.**

Commissioning

One: The Cross confronts us.

All: **It shows that unrestrained power can lead to death.**

One: The Cross invites us

All: **To walk the Christian path which calls for sacrifice.**

One: The Cross challenges us,

All: **Not just to observe suffering, but to relieve it.**

One: The Cross leaves us in awe.

All: **The love of God goes beyond all limits.**

Easter Sunday

Acts 10:34–43 or Isaiah 65:17–25
Psalm 118:1–2, 14–24
1 Corinthians 15:19–26 or Acts 10:34–43
John 20:1–18 or Luke 24:1–12

Call to Worship

One: The discovery of courageous women at the tomb.
All: "Jesus is risen!"
One: The voices of astounded disciples.
All: "He is risen!"
One: The joyful cry of Easter Christians down the ages.
All: "Christ is risen!"
One: Joy beyond joy; hope beyond hope; love beyond love;
yes, Christ is risen!
All: He is risen indeed! Alleluia!

Or

Call to Worship

One: There is surprise.
All: Christ is risen!
One: There is wonder.
All: Christ is risen!
One: There is joy.
All: Christ is risen!
One: There is restored community.
All: Christ is risen!
One: God's love is there.
All: Christ is risen indeed!

Easter Opening Prayer

One: This is the day of new life.

All: **Christ has broken free from death.**

One: This is the day of limitless opportunity.

All: **The power that was nailed to the Cross has been released.**

One: This is the day of renewed community.

All: **In worship and through service,**
we are one in Jesus Christ.

One: This is the day of wonderful celebration.

All: **God's love has suffered but won through;**
God's love is forever with us and for us! Amen.

Prayer of Affirmation and Reflection

One: Easter takes us on a new journey.

All: **The narrow paths we followed,**
the restricting patterns of life, no longer bind us.

One: Easter opens up new horizons for us.

All: **The limits that held us back, the deadening opinions of others, no**
longer have power over us.

One: Easter renews and restores us.

All: **We have escaped from the groove of tradition,**
broken free from the hold of prejudice.

One: Easter enables us to see the world with new eyes.

All: **Our reluctance to work justly, our reluctance to stand beside the**
powerless, is over for good.

One: Easter has given us God's love in the Risen Christ.

All: **Now we can experience that love in action.**
Now we can feel that love transforming each day for ourselves.
(Time for silent reflection)

Or

Easter Prayer of Affirmation and Confession

One: You bring us out from the tombs in which we have been buried.

All: **From the tomb of apathy you bring us to action,**
from the tomb of guilt you bring us to a fresh start,

from the tomb of uncaring you bring us to compassion,
from the tomb of self-focus you bring us to generosity,
from the tomb of fear you bring us to faith.
   (Time for silent reflection)

Words of Assurance

One: We rise to new life in Christ
All: **As we walk with freedom and confidence.**
One: We rise to new life in Christ
All: **As we refuse to compromise with the truth.**
One: We rise to new life in Christ
All: **As talents are used to promote justice and inclusiveness.**
One: We rise to new life in Christ
All: **As we take the lifestyle of Jesus as our example.**
One: God's peace is yours; God's pardon sets you free!
All: **Thanks be to God! Amen.**

Offering Prayer

One: There is new life in these gifts, O God:
All: **A promise of joy to the downhearted,**
   a sense of hope to the sorrowing,
   a renewal of courage for the powerless,
   a way to Christ's love for the faithless.
One: Bless these gifts, O God, and bless those who work with them. Amen.

Commissioning

One: The risen Spirit of Jesus is with us as we leave this church,
All: **Renewing our worship,**
   binding us in Christian community,
   encouraging us to use our varied gifts,
   calling us to stand up and be counted.
One: In the spirit of Christ, everything is possible!
All: **Fear and death are defeated. Alleluia!**

2nd Sunday of Easter

Acts 5:27–32
Psalm 118:14–29 or Psalm 150
Revelation 1:4–8
John 20:19–31

Call to Worship

One: Binding us into community,
All: **Christ is among us!**
One: Banishing our doubts,
All: **Christ is among us!**
One: Ending our fears,
All: **Christ is among us!**
One: Bringing us hope,
All: **Christ is among us!**

Opening Prayer

One: We have not seen Jesus, but we believe!
All: **We believe he welcomes our questions and our doubts.**
One: We have not seen Jesus, but we believe!
All: **We believe he calls us to create accepting communities.**
One: We have not seen Jesus but we believe!
All: **We believe he encourages us to act justly and to promote healing.**
One: We have not seen Jesus, but we believe!
All: **We believe; he inspires us to spread the life-giving Good News wherever we go. Amen.**

Prayer of Confession

One: Living God, you have placed the Risen Christ in our midst.
All: **Our apathy and uncaring falls away.**
One: Living God, you have placed the Risen Christ in our midst.
All: **Our priorities fall easily into place.**
One: Living God, you have placed the Risen Christ in our midst.

All: Our doubts are faced, our uncertainties put in a faith perspective.

One: Living God, you have placed the Risen Christ in our midst.

All: We are ready to look beyond our homes and local church, to support and to reconcile.

One: Living God, you have placed the Risen Christ in our midst.

All: We realize that death has been defeated, and the limits of time overcome.

(Time for silent reflection)

Or

Prayer of Confession

One: O God, composer of the galaxies and of our world, we praise you.

All: When we fail to honor your creation, forgive us!

One: O God, whose peaceful melodies touch the hearts of those who are troubled, we worship you.

All: When we fail to create harmony, forgive us!

One: O God, instrument of peace and justice, we glorify you.

All: When our words and actions are out of tune with your world, forgive us!

One: O God, whose supreme work was known in Jesus Christ, we adore you.

All: When we fail to practice compassion,
when our discipleship does not resonate with your love,
forgive us.

(Time for silent reflection)

Words of Assurance

One: "Peace be with you."

All: The fear that has held us bound, falls away.

One: "Peace be with you."

All: The joy we find in community comes home to us.

One: "Peace be with you."

All: We are enabled to reach out beyond neighborhood and nation.

One: "Peace be with you."

All: **We have peace through the Holy Spirit.**
We may bring forgiving peace through the same Spirit.
One: Peace, peace, peace be with you!

Offering Prayer

One: We bring to you our Easter hope, O God,
All: **Confident that compassion will be encouraged**
and doubts faced;
One: Confident that young persons will be supported,
those of advanced years honored, and the distressed upheld;
All: **Confident that the saving work of Jesus**
will continually grow – locally, nationally, and globally.
One: Bless these our hopeful gifts, O God,
and enliven our spirit of giving. Amen.

Or

Offering Prayer (together)

All: **We are your gifted people, O God.**
You have given us talent of mind, and heart, and spirit.
You have put joy in our hearts and on our lips.
As you have blessed us with so much that is good,
so bless these gifts which symbolize our faithfulness,
in the name of Jesus Christ. Amen.

Commissioning

One: We leave this church, O God,
with songs of new life on our lips,
All: **With a message of hope in our hearts,**
with a determination to serve on our minds,
with the love of Jesus Christ
binding us together in faith community.

Or

Commissioning

One: Doubts cannot hold us.

All: Fear cannot bind us.

One: Apathy cannot subdue us.

All: Death cannot defeat us.

One: Love cannot reject us.

All: Time cannot capture us.

One: Christ is for us.

All: God will eternally secure us.

3rd Sunday of Easter

Acts 9:1–6, (7–20)
Psalm 30
Revelation 5:11–14
John 21:1–19

Call to Worship

One: Risen in joy,

All: We come before you, God, and rejoice.

One: Risen in hope,

All: We come before you, God, in anticipation.

One: Risen in love,

All: We come before you, God, with thankful hearts.

One: Risen for the world,

All: We come before you, God, in solidarity with all your suffering people. Amen.

Opening Prayer

One: You call us from family life, from school, and from work, O God,

All: To the joy and inspiration of worship.

One: You call us from concern about our world, and concern about our-selves, O God,

All: To the joy and inspiration of Jesus Christ, the peace-bringer.

One: You call us from dwelling on our yesterdays, from dreading the future, from counting our losses,

All: To the joy and inspiration of this supportive faith community.

One: Bless our praise, bless our prayers, bless our reflections on your Word, O God,

All: That we may know new life in Jesus Christ, and bring new life to others. Amen.

Prayer of Confession

One: When we are caught up in our own importance,

All: **Give us a vision of Peter, who was humbled in Pilate's courtyard.**

One: When we are lacking in self-confidence,

All: **Give us a vision of the disciples in the Upper Room, encouraged by the Risen Jesus.**

One: When we feel disheartened, and without hope,

All: **Give us a vision of the disciples fishing on the lake, elated when Jesus brought success to them.**

One: When we can only see one point of view, when we are closed to new truth,

All: **Give us a vision of Saul on the Damascus Road, encountering Jesus whom he had persecuted.**

(Time for silent reflection)

Words of Assurance

One: A change in attitude, a change in perspective, a change from inaction, a change to faithfulness, a renewal of community, are all possible for those touched by the Risen Christ.

All: **We are ready for change!**

One: The pardon and peace of Christ are yours!

All: **Thanks be to God! Amen.**

Offering Prayer

One: God, Giver of all, we return to you our gifts.

All: **As you have given graciously,**
as you have shared generously,
as you have forgiven freely,
as you have cared compassionately,
so bless our gifts,
for we offer them in the name of your Blessed One, Jesus. Amen.

Commissioning

One: Find Jesus unexpectedly!

All: We find him at the moment of greatest aloneness.

One: Find Jesus joyfully!

All: We find him in the midst of a family celebration.

One: Find Jesus gratefully!

All: We find him when calm comes in the midst of crisis.

One: Find Jesus in faith community!

All: We find him as we work with others for justice and freedom.

One: Find Jesus eternally!

All: We will find him, when our time merges with God's time.

4th Sunday of Easter

Acts 9:36–43
Psalm 23
Revelation 7:9–17
John 10:22–30

Call to Worship

One: This is the place of gathering.

All: We gather to celebrate God's love.

One: This is place of praise-bringing.

All: We praise God for gifts wonderful and gracious.

One: This is the place of listening.

All: We listen for God's life-giving Word to inspire and lead us.

One: This is the place for building faith community.

All: Joined in community, we can work for God's justice and bring God's peace.

Opening Prayer

One: The Good Shepherd brings us together.

All: With joy, we join in community to worship and serve.

One: As the Shepherd has known rejection, yet you our God care for us.

All: When the storm rages, in the midst of the struggle, we will be secure.

One: As the Shepherd has known adversity, yet you our God lead us.

All: In a maze of tough choices, through the darkest night, our Guide will show us the Way.

One: The Shepherd has known hatred and abuse, yet you our God, keep on loving.

All: In life, in death, our Beloved will bring us home. Amen.

Prayer of Confession

One: You reveal yourself in many ways, O God.
     Many images help us to understand your special significance to us.
     You reveal yourself as Shepherd.

All: **When we ignore your wise call, when we go our own way,**
       forgive us!

One: You reveal yourself as Gracious Host.

All: **When we turn down your invitation,**
       when we focus on the faults of our fellow guests,
       forgive us!

One: You reveal yourself as Friend.

All: **When we rely only on our own resources,**
       when our pride refuses freely offered help,
       forgive us!

One: You reveal yourself as Courage-bringer to the powerless;

All: **When we will not recognize the needy,**
       when we fail to support the downtrodden,
       forgive us!

   (Time for silent reflection)

Words of Assurance

One: Like lost sheep, we have strayed off the straight and narrow way,
       O God; we have let you down.

All: **But you know us beyond our imagining,**
       you know us through and through,
       you will not keep us in the dark and pointless places.

One: You put us on our feet again;
       you bring us back to the right road.

All: **You will inspire us to stand up to those who insult and criticize.**

One: You stay with us when the tempting times return.

All: **We are ready to follow you, our Shepherd leader.**

One: Pardon and peace are yours.

All: **Thanks be to God! Amen.**

Or

Words of Assurance

One: It is our apathy that keeps us from your way, O God;
it is a lack of faith in our abilities, which holds us back.
Your Loving Spirit will change us, free us, motivate us for good.

All: **We are ready to let the Holy Spirit go to work with us.**

One: Know the peace and presence of God.

All: **To God be thanks and praise! Amen.**

Offering Prayer

One: Graciously you have given to us, O God;
graciously we return your gifts and ask you to bless them.

All: **The gifts of money, may we use wisely;**
the gifts of skill and talent, may we use creatively and
compassionately;
the gift of time, may we use carefully;
the gift of faith, may we use joyfully.

One: For we pray in the name of Jesus Christ, your supreme gift to our
world. Amen.

Or

Offering Prayer

One: Accept our gifts, O God, as they are used in your service.

All: **Worship is made possible through them**
and through them hope comes alive.

One: Dreams become reality through these gifts,
and through them children grow in faith.

All: **Bless this money;**
bless our gifts of energy, time, and friendship
in the name of Jesus Christ. Amen.

Or

Offering Prayer

One: These gifts, O God, will help people get back on the right paths.

All: **The sick, on the path of healing;**
The distressed on the path to wholeness;
The disturbed on the path to peace;
And the powerless on the path to self-confidence.

One: Bless all that we offer in Christ's name,
and give us, O God, the courage to take the new paths,
which will bring honor to your Holy Name. Amen.

Commissioning

One: Follow the Good Shepherd

All: **Into ways of truth and justice.**

One: Listen to the Good Shepherd

All: **For wise words that can be trusted.**

One: Believe in the Good Shepherd

All: **For a faith that cannot be shaken.**

One: Be challenged by the Good Shepherd

All: **To change your friends and your community with love.**

Or

Commissioning

One: The Good Shepherd cares for the sheep;
God cares for you who are the children of God.

All: **We trust God's Word.**
Its truth has been proved over the generations.
We trust God's Holy One, Jesus.
His Way is enlightening and practical.
We trust the community of faith.
It is determined to support, encourage, and serve.

One: Trust your Christian identity;
it will hold you strong in the storms of life.

5th Sunday of Easter

(Some of the options are intended for celebration as Family Sunday.)

Acts 11:1–18
Psalm 148
Revelation 21:1–6
John 13:31–35

Call to Worship *(loudly and with feeling)*

One: The chorus of morning birdsong proclaims it;
the grandeur of the mountains displays it.
All: **The glory of God, the glory of God!**
One: The laughter of playing children affirms it;
the warmth of a mother with her baby reflects it.
All: **The glory of God, the glory of God!**
One: The relief of a refugee finding a country sighs it;
the joy of the unemployed person finding a job, shouts it out loud.
All: **The glory of God, the glory of God!**
One: God in Highest Heaven, God at home with humankind.
All: **The glory of God, the glory of God!**

Opening Prayer

One: With the loving vulnerability of a tiny baby,
All: **We open ourselves to you, O God.**
One: With the infinite curiosity of a growing child,
All: **We search for you, O God.**
One: With the joyful responsibility of young parents,
All: **We rely on you, O God.**
One: With the reflective experience of maturity,
All: **We sense your presence, O God.**
One: With the creaking wisdom of advancing years,
All: **We rest in a hope strong and secure, O God.**
In all our living, in all our striving, in all our forgiving,
to you we look, eternally present One. Amen.

A Confessional Prayer for Family Sunday

One: Deepen our understanding of family, O God,

**All: That we may perceive the hidden hurt,
encourage the neglected talent,
and meet the unspoken need.**

One: Widen our understanding of family, O God,

**All: That we may support the powerless stranger,
recognize our struggling neighbor,
and identify the lonely newcomer.**

One: Make holy our understanding of family, O God,

**All: That your light may defeat the darkness,
Christ's acceptance mark our relationships,
and the Spirit renew our faith community.**

  (Time for silent reflection)

Words of Assurance

One: Life within families, the human family and the family of Jesus Christ, requires reflection, commitment, and hard, faithful work. Are you willing to grow and to mature in your family life?

All: We are willing.

One: God grants you pardon, peace, and new beginnings.

All: Thanks be to God! Amen.

Or

Prayer of Confession for Family Sunday *(based on words of Jesus)*

One: "I give you a new commandment... As I have loved you, you also should love one another."

All: It isn't easy, O God, to love those who bad-mouth you, and hold grudges against you.

One "I give you a new commandment... As I have loved you, you also should love one another."

All: It isn't easy, O God, to love those who are prejudiced, and will not see another person's point of view.

One "I give you a new commandment... As I have loved you, you also should love one another."

All: It isn't easy, O God, to love those who will not move from "the way it's always been done," and rejoice in new ways.

One   "I give you a new commandment... As I have loved you, you also should love one another."

All: It isn't easy, O God, to love those whose vision is restricted to the community, and will not encompass local and global concerns.

One   "I give you a new commandment... As I have loved you, you also should love one another."

  (Time for silent reflection)

Words of Assurance *(based on words of Paul)*

One: "Love is patient... love does not insist on its own way."

All: **As we listen, O God, as we refuse to judge,**
your love comes home to us.

One: "Love is kind, it is not boastful or arrogant."

All: **As we reflect, O God, as we put ourselves in the other person's**
shoes, your love comes home to us.

One: "Love is not irritable or resentful;
it does not insist on having its own way."

All: **As we take positive action to bring change, as Jesus did, O God,**
your love comes home to us.

One: Pardon and peace are yours.

All: **Thanks be to God. Amen.**

Offering Prayer

One: Loving God, you have blessed us with the gift of family,

All: **To laugh with us, to listen to us, to comfort us, and**
to stay beside us.

One: Bless these, our gifts, that through them

All: **The troubled may smile again,**
the anxious may be comforted,
the needy may be cared for,
and the vulnerable may know security.

One: This is the Way of Jesus.

All: **Thanks be to God! Amen.**

Commissioning

One: We are ready to show our responsibility, as a member of the diverse family of humankind.

All: **We are committed to reflect, worship, and serve, as a member of the Christian family.**

One: We rejoice in the love, security, and responsibility, which is ours as members of the human family.

All: **We will stand beside those family members who are tested, afraid, or have suffered loss.**

Or

Commissioning

One: Live joyfully in your families!

All: **We will listen to the deepest needs.**
We will encourage the downhearted.
We will discover hidden talent.
We will reconcile the feuding.
We will secure the vulnerable.
We will protect the innocent.
We will confront the disturbers.
We will cherish the fragile.

One: Give yourself to the needs of the wider family circle.
Do everything in the lively Spirit of Jesus Christ.

6th Sunday of Easter

Acts 16:9–15
Psalm 67
Revelation 21:10, 22 – 22:5
John 14:23–29 or John 5:1–9

Call to Worship

One: Joyful praise, is God's promise.

All: Music and song will gladden our hearts in worship.

One: Inspiration from the scriptures, is God's promise.

All: Through our listening and reflection, God's Word will come alive.

One: Faith community friendship, is God's promise.

All: As we build each other up, Christ's family will prosper.

One: The loving Spirit, is God's promise.

All: The Spirit will lead us to the peace that nothing can destroy.

Opening Prayer

One: The Holy Spirit is our helper.

All: The Spirit will guide us when we cannot find the way.

One: The Holy Spirit is our encourager.

All: The Spirit will support us when the future seems bleak.

One: The Holy Spirit is our comforter.

All: The Spirit will be there for us when loss hits home.

One: The Holy Spirit is our peace-bringer.

All: The Spirit will break through hostility with a loving power.

Or

Opening Prayer

One: We gather from the anxiety and the struggle of our everyday life.

All: We come to seek God's peaceful presence.

One: We gather from a world where violence and the images of conflict are all around us.

All: We come to be a part of a peaceful community.

One: We gather with unresolved concerns and fears that worry us.

All: **We come to find the "peace of God which passes all human under-standing."**

One: We gather under the name of the One who was a peace-bringer and a peacemaker.

All: **We come as followers and disciples of Jesus Christ, who is the Way of peace. Amen.**

Prayer of Confession

One: God shows us that we can go beyond our self-imposed limits.

All: **As we open ourselves to new truth,**
as we try out new skills and test new relationships,
God goes with us.

One: God strengthens us in unforeseen ways.

All: **In our acceptance of new realities,**
in our commitment to reflect and to begin again,
God goes with us.

One: God will reveal unfaithful ways of daily living.

All: **As we become aware of a mean and selfish spirit,**
and as we turn to compassion and giving,
God is with us.

One: God broadens our horizons.

All: **In our active concern for the poor and powerless,**
in our neighborhood and in our world,
God is with us.

(Time for silent reflection)

Words of Assurance

One: As we align our vision with God's vision,

All: **The past comes into perspective and the future is clear.**

One: Know joy, pardon and peace, as you begin in a new way.

All: **Thanks be to God. Amen!**

Or

Words of Assurance

One: God calls us not to overburden ourselves with guilt, nor yet to pass over our faults lightly;

All: **God calls us to a faithful response,
as we reflect on our shortcomings,
and plan for a new way in the future.
Our peace-bringing God will not let us down!
God is with us as we hear the words of pardon, and as we begin anew.**

One: You are accepted, you are forgiven, thanks be to God!

All: **Amen.**

Offering Prayer

One: These gifts which we bring to you, O God, to bless, are our peace offering.

All: **They will be effective, as the sick and the needy among us know peace.
They will be effective, as this faith community becomes "an instrument of your peace."
They will be effective as those, far from this place, experience healing communities and proclaim justice by word and deed – your shalom!**

One: And the effectiveness of these gifts will have the mark of Jesus Christ about them!

All: **Amen.**

Commissioning

One: Know the peace of God.

All: **Confront your fears.**

One: Know the peace of God.

All: **Be ready to forgive.**

One: Know the peace of God.

All: **Speak out for truth and justice.**

One: Know the peace of God.

All: **Follow Christ who brings lasting peace.**

7th Sunday of Easter

Acts 16:16–34
Psalm 97
Revelation 22:12–14, 16–17, 20–21
John 17:20–26

Call to Worship

One: We come into your presence, O God,

All: Though we find it difficult to leave our pressing concerns behind.

One: We come into your presence,
and we remember how much we have to thank you for.

**All: We look up at the star-filled heavens,
we experience a laughing child at play,
and our thanksgiving is wholehearted.**

One: We come into your presence,
and we rejoice in this worship-willing faith community.

**All: As the prayers are offered, praise sung,
the peace passed, and the Word read,
we know we are faithfully at home.**

One: We come into your presence knowing
that you call us to listen and to act.

**All: The need to encourage the troubled is before us,
the opportunity to support those lacking in self-confidence is clear
to us.**

Opening

One: We will follow your lead, O God.

**All: The choice of paths is before us,
but you mark out the faithful one for us.**

One: We will follow your lead, O God.

**All: You show us the compassionate way,
and give us good companions for the journey.**

One: We will follow your lead, O God.

All: **In moments of celebration, in the testing days,**
you are there for us.

One: We will follow your lead, O God.

All: **For in Jesus Christ, you have shown us**
what it means to respond wholeheartedly
to your leading. Amen.

Or

Opening

One: The world rejoices!

All: **The glory of God shines in the morning sunrise,**
and sings with the dawn chorus.

One: The world rejoices!

All: **The influence of Jesus Christ is abroad,**
as the sick are healed and the downtrodden feel new confidence.

One: The world rejoices!

All: **The Holy Spirit goes to work;**
those who have suffered loss receive hope;
the doubting know faith.

One: The world rejoices!

All: **And we who are citizens of the world,**
join the song of joy. Amen.

Prayer for Insight

One: When a friend says, "Nothing is wrong, I'll be all right,"

All: **Give us the patience to stay with them,**
give us the courage to hear their deepest anxieties.

One: When the pressure is on to take a difficult decision,

All: **Give us the wisdom to take our time,**
and the strength to weigh our alternatives carefully.

One: When we cannot forget a hurt, or forgive a telling slight,

All: **Enable us to see the other person's point of view,**
and put the past in the past.

One: When the call to justice is heard,
and the demand to act comes loud and clear,

All: **Give us the willingness to listen,
and the faithful Gospel response,
which may not be comfortable.**
      (Time for silent reflection)

Words of Assurance

One: God will enable you to see new truth and to set out on a fresh path.

All: **We will take the time to consider our failings;
we will work to change things for good.**

One: God's peace will be yours.

All: **Thanks be to God! Amen.**

Or

A Prayer of Hope *(based on the words of Jesus)*

One: Jesus prayed, "that they all may be one," O God. We look for the time
when the whole world will be one, in concern for the weakest and
poorest, for the very old and the very young.

All: **We pray that we will find a role in this huge task; a gift, a message,
an active form of participation.**

One: Jesus prayed, "that all may be one," O God. We pray that the communities of faith will unite in sharing their beliefs and working for
common goals.

All: **We pray that we might play a part in this task, a contact, a discussion, a work project.**

One: Jesus prayed, "that they may all be one," O God. We pray that neighborhood groups will get together to care for those most vulnerable and
at risk.

All: **We pray that our faith community may join with others, to offer a
meeting place, to provide leadership, and be the focus for expressed hopes and just demands.**
      (Time for silent reflection)

Words of Assurance

One: Together, we are able to do so much more than on our own.
We know, O God, that you will bless our common endeavors.

All: In our willingness to listen to the beliefs of others,
in our ability to respond to the dreams of others,
in our readiness to inspire change for others,
in our preparedness to work for justice with others,

One: The spirit of Jesus is alive, and at work.

All: And your peace, O God, will be our peace. Amen.

Offering Prayer

One: Graciously you have given to us, O God.
Graciously we return your gifts. We ask you to bless them as we strive
for unity.

All: May these gifts of money be used to show our solidarity with those
of other faith communities.

One: May our gifts of skill and talent bring us together in common tasks for
the relief of suffering.

All: May our gift of faith be shared carefully with those whose beliefs
are different from our own.

One: We pray in the name of Jesus, your glorious gift to the world, O God.
Amen.

Commissioning

One: Pray for the world, that its leaders will get their act together, that we will be one in our concern for all humankind.

All: **We pray that the air, the water, and the whole earth will be protected for our grandchildren.**

One: We pray that the peacemakers find a way to achieve peace.

All: **We pray that women will have the same opportunities as men.**

One: We pray that children will get the food, clothes, and shelter they need, without regard to their country of origin.

All: **We pray that the dignity of regular work will be there, for each person who wants to work;**

One: We pray that those who choose to worship, will be able to do so according to their faith tradition. In the name of the One God, we pray.

All: **Amen.**

Pentecost Sunday

Acts 2:1–21 or Genesis 11:1–9
Psalm 104:24–34, 35b
Romans 8:14–17 or Acts 2:1–21
John 14:8–17, (25–27)

Call to Worship *(inspired by Psalm 104:24–34)*

One: Come let us praise the Giver of life.
All: The earth is filled with God's creatures.
One: Come let us praise the Sustainer of life.
**All: The air, the waters, the moving changing universe,
have their continued existence in God.**
One: Come let us praise the Renewer of life.
**All: God's love casts out fear;
God's justice gives confidence to the powerless.**
One: Come let us praise the Eternal Life-bringer.
All: God's glorious realm has no beginning and no end.

Or

Call to Worship

One: A rushing, violent windstorm –
All: The Spirit is here!
One: The moving, startling tongues of fire –
All: The Spirit is empowering!
One: The gathered, inspired followers of Jesus –
**All: The Spirit brings us together hopefully,
and will send us out faithfully!**

Opening Prayer

One: With the inspiring, life-giving Spirit, there is always worship,
**All: Worship that sings, worship that soars,
worship that comes home to us.**

One: With the inspiring, life-giving Spirit, there is always community,

All: Community that sees need, community that is compassionate, community that reaches out.

One: With the inspiring, life-giving Spirit, there are always new opportunities,

All: Opportunities to serve, opportunities to use talents, opportunities to respond to God's call.

One: With the inspiring, life-giving Spirit, there is always the Way of Jesus Christ,

**All: A way of justice, a way that includes everyone in, a simple way of love.
Stay with us, inspiring, life-giving, Holy Spirit,
for with you everything is possible. Amen.**

Or

Opening Prayer

One: Soaring, flowing, questing, dancing…

All: The Holy Spirit leads us to praise.

One: Searching, finding, changing, challenging…

All: The Holy Spirit calls us to faithfulness.

One: Gently, calmly, simply, persistently…

All: The Holy Spirit invites us to reflection.

One: With perseverance, with encouragement, with joy, with urgency…

All: The Holy Spirit moves us to action.

Prayer of Confession

One: On the Day of Pentecost, the faith community turned from hopelessness to joy.

All: May the breath of renewal come into our fellowship, O God, to bring us together, and to send us out to serve.

One: On the Day of Pentecost, the barriers between Jews and Gentiles and Greeks came tumbling down.

All: May the breath of renewal bring us closer to those whom we look on with suspicion, O God, and those of whom we are afraid.

One: On the Day of Pentecost, the disciples found their voice and gained self-confidence.

All: **May the breath of renewal show us gifts long hidden, O God, and give us the ability to use them.**

One: On the Day of Pentecost, a spirit of generosity filled the church.

All: **May the breath of renewal enable us to give beyond self-imposed limits, O God, and enable us to break through them.**

(Time for silent reflection)

Words of Assurance

One: The Holy Spirit frees us.

All: **Life-bringing Holy Spirit, give us light in our darkness; give us strength in our weakness; give us gentleness in our resolve; give us peace in our struggling; give us love in and through all things.**

One: Know pardon and the way of new life in Jesus Christ.

All: **Thanks be to God! Amen.**

Offering Prayer

One: Seeing Spirit, searching Spirit, need-sensing Spirit, need-meeting Spirit,

All: **Generous Spirit, sharing Spirit, Holy Spirit,**

One: Bless these gifts, and all the gifts of heart and mind used in the service of the church.

All: **Amen.**

Commissioning

One: We leave this church, overflowing with Spirit joy,

All: **On fire with the love of God,**

One: Sensing the firm support of our faith community,

All: **Enthusiastic for the Good News of Jesus Christ,**

One: Ready to work with the Holy Spirit in the world.

Trinity Sunday
1st Sunday after Pentecost

Proverbs 8:1–4, 22–31
Psalm 8
Romans 5:1–5
John 16:12–15

Call to Worship
One: Creator God; forming the oceans, raising the mountains, author of the smallest cell,
All: **We worship you!**
One: Jesus Christ; Loved One of God, infinitely faithful, cruelly crucified, wonderfully risen,
All: **We adore you!**
One: Holy Spirit; Influence of God, unseen but present, working purposefully, eternally compassionate,
All: **We glorify you!**

Opening Prayer *(based on Romans 5:1)*
One: The God of Peace
All: **Calls us to worship together.**
One: The God of Peace
All: **Calls us to listen to God's Word carefully, and act faithfully.**
One: The God of Peace
All: **Calls us to value church members, young and old, equally.**
One: The God of Peace
All: **Calls us to create peace sensitively,**
     and to maintain peace enthusiastically,
     in our homes, in our faith community, in our turbulent world.
One: We have peace with God through Jesus Christ.
All: **Amen.**

Prayer of Confession

One: A model of endurance, in the face of threats;

All: **Moses, resisting the Egyptian king.**

One: A model of faithful friendship, in testing circumstances;

All: **Ruth, going to Naomi's homeland.**

One: A model of speaking out, when injustice is clear;

All: **Amos, drawing attention to a corrupt society.**

One: A model of acceptance, and sacrificial caring;

All: **Jesus, living and dying in obedience to God's will.**

(Time for silent reflection)

Words of Assurance

One: Pardon and peace are your gifts, O God,

All: **When we endure faithfully, speak out fearlessly,**
and show a spirit of generosity, consistently. Amen.

Prayer of Dedication

One: The one true God is known, as our gifts refresh the local faith community.

All: **Jesus Christ is known, as our gifts are used**
to bring different churches together, for worship and for service.

One: The Holy Spirit is known, as our gifts bring joy and empowerment, to communities and churches, way beyond this nation.

Commissioning

All: **May the love of God, wonderful creator, eternal sustainer,**
embrace you.
May the love of Christ, instrument of compassion, advocate for
justice, affirm you.
May the love of the Holy Spirit, giver of courage, giver of hope,
work with you.

Sunday between
June 12 and 18 inclusive

Proper 6 [11]

1 Kings 21:1–10, (11–14), 15–21a
Psalm 5:1–8
Galatians 2:15–21
Luke 7:36 – 8:3

Call to Worship

One: The welcoming approach of Jesus Christ
All: **Becomes our welcome, to all who worship in this church.**
One: The inspiring words of Jesus Christ
All: **Become our words of assurance and forgiveness,**
  and our call to avoid a judgmental stance.
One: The faithful way of Jesus Christ
All: **Becomes our way of acceptance and challenge,**
  and our concern for the powerless and depressed.
One: The compassionate ministry of Jesus Christ
All: **Becomes our response to his sacrifice on the cross,**
  our ministry of healing, listening, and care.
One: Let us worship God!

Opening Prayer

One: Unending is your faithfulness, O God.
All: **From the beginnings of history, you have been with your creation.**
One: Inspiring is your faithfulness, O God.
All: **From generation to generation, you have looked for us and found**
  us in this church family.
One: Awesome is your faithfulness, O God.
All: **In the midst of life's trials and turmoils, you have been a rock, the**
  One on whom we can rely.
One: A saving grace is your faithfulness, O God.

All: In Jesus Christ your faithfulness has become clear.
Through Jesus we are enabled to faithfully serve the youngest ones, the needy persons, and those of advanced years. Amen.

Prayer of Confession

One: We are quick to see the faults and failings of others, slow to admit to our own shortcomings.

All: **Gracious God, open our eyes.**

One: We are quick to make clear our own achievements and successes, slow to affirm others in their times of achievement.

All: **Gracious God, make us confidence builders.**

One: We are quick to point out those aspects of church life which need changing, slow to offer our commitment to the life of the faith community.

All: **Gracious God, unite us in service.**

One: We are quick to appreciate the faith and witness of this local congregation, slow to open our hearts to the life of the wider church.

All: **Gracious God, broaden our vision.**

   (Time for silent reflection)

Or

A Prayer of Reflection

One: A woman with sinful past comes to visit Jesus.

All: **Jesus meets her without judgment or prejudice.
Would we have welcomed her attention?**

One: The woman anoints Jesus with costly ointment.

All: **Would we have appreciated her generosity,
or suggested the money could have been used for charitable purposes?**

One: The Pharisee is surprised that Jesus has welcomed her loving act.

All: **Do we not judge people by their reputation,
and by the company they keep?**

One: Jesus held up her action as an example of compassion,
and was quick to make clear that her sins had been forgiven.

All:　Would we have seen the woman in such a compassionate light, and would we have been as ready to offer her forgiveness?
　　　(Time for silent reflection)

Words of Assurance

One:　You are ready to open our eyes, O God, to another point of view; you will deal gently with our judgment and prejudice.

All:　**You call us to have done with labeling,**
　　　and to be open to the insights of some surprising people.

One:　This is the way of renewal. God accepts your change of heart.

All:　**Thanks be to God. Amen.**

Or

Words of Assurance

One:　Gracious God, you gift us with the will to change our lives for good.

All:　**With the ability to deal with temptation, you have gifted us;**
　　　with the ability to appreciate spontaneous generosity, you have
　　　gifted us;
　　　with the ability to see people with new eyes, you have gifted us;
　　　with the ability to forgive ourselves and others, you have gifted us;
　　　with the ability to participate in the work of Jesus Christ, you have
　　　gifted us.

One:　Through God's grace you are forgiven, and freed to live and work as followers of Jesus Christ.

All:　**Thanks be to God. Amen.**

Offering Prayer

One: You know us, O God, by the way we give.

All: **In our willingness to understand the church's needs, you know our concern;**

in our sharing for the poor, the compromised and the rejected, you know our generosity;

in our desire to spread the Good News, in word and deed, you know our priorities.

One: Bless these gifts, O God, and touch these gathered givers, lovingly and peacefully. Amen.

Commissioning

One: The Holy Spirit is with us!

All: **The Word is our inspiration.**

One: The Holy Spirit is with us!

All: **The faith community takes heart.**

One: The Holy Spirit is with us!

All: **We move into challenging territory.**

One: The Holy Spirit is with us!

All: **We have nothing to fear.**

Sunday between
June 19 and 25 inclusive

Proper 7 [12]

1 Kings 19:1–15a
Psalm 42 and 43
Galatians 3:23–29
Luke 8:26–39

Call to Worship

One: Out of an awesome thankfulness for the gift of our world, and for the gift of life itself,

All: **We gather to praise your name, wonderful Creator God.**

One: Out of profound thankfulness for the gift of the church, and for the faith community in this place,

All: **We gather to hear your Word for us, Living God.**

One: Out of a humble thankfulness for the gift of your Chosen One, Jesus Christ, and the opportunity to serve him faithfully,

All: **We gather as his followers, and will work in his loving Way, Eternal God.**

Opening Prayer

One: In a spirit of joyful hope we offer our prayers to you, O God.

All: **You accept us as we are; you hear our deepest concerns.**

One: In a spirit of gentle compassion,
we offer our prayers to you, O God.

All: **You open our hearts to the suffering ones
and equip us to meet their needs.**

One: In a spirit of common participation,
we offer our prayers to you, O God.

All: **You alert us to our common responsibilities;
you enable us to meet challenges together.**

One: In a spirit of justice, we offer our prayers to you, O God.

All: You will not let the powerless be walked over;
you will encourage us to stand beside those
who have the least. Amen.

Prayer of Confession

One: You bring us to the city dump, O God; you show us huge quantities of
paper, plastic, and glass which could be recycled.

All: **You challenge us to act, and to speak out, in a way that will**
preserve the resources of our fragile planet.

One: You bring us to the emergency department of the local hospital and
show us patients lying on temporary beds.

All: **You encourage us to speak out against reduction in health funding;**
you encourage us to give our loved ones the practical and spiritual
support that they need.

One: You bring us to the kitchen of a city home and show us a group of
friends and family members. Some are arguing, some look lonely.

All: **You remind us of all we can do to restore friendship, and to**
promote acceptance of those who feel they are "on the outside."

One: You bring us to the basement of a local church and show us the
congregation having coffee after the service. There are newcomers
needing a listening ear, young persons seeking attention.

All: **You alert us of the need to welcome, and of the call to serve**
persons of all ages in the name of Jesus Christ.
(Time for silent reflection)

Words of Assurance

One: You give us eyes to see the reality of our world, our friends, even
ourselves, O God, and you give us the power to make changes that are
in accord with the Way of Jesus Christ.

All: **We are ready to challenge the accepted order of things,**
to promote reconciliation, and to turn around
some of the selfish and mean spirited ways that are ours.

One: Then receive God's pardon and peace!

All: **Thanks be to God! Amen.**

Offering Prayer

One: Loving God, help us to give to you,
in the Spirit you have given to us,

All: **With a generosity beyond imagining,**
with a sense of justice that will not rest,
with a desire to forgive that is unrelenting,
with a breadth of vision that is global,
and with a love that you made clear to us in Jesus. Amen.

Commissioning

One: Look sensitively, and realize your influence for good.

All: **Look around, and know what you can achieve with other members**
of the church.

One: Look with humility, and wonder at what God has done and will do for
you.

All: **Look thankfully, and realize what God has given you.**

One: Look practically, and see the work you can do for God and God's
purposes.

All: **Look graciously and know that God loves you beyond all time and**
all imagining.

Sunday between
June 26 and July 2 inclusive

Proper 8 [13]

2 Kings 2:1–2, 6–14
Psalm 77:1–2, 11–20
Galatians 5:1, 13–25
Luke 9:51–62

Call to Worship

One: God of times past, God of our present days,
      God of all the days that are to come,
All: You are with us.
One: Celebrating with us in the joyful times,
      supporting us in times of loss,
All: You are with us.
One: Encouraging us to have done with injustice,
      encouraging us to embrace new truth,
All: You are with us.
One: The object and focus of our worship,
      the inspiration of our praise and prayer,
All: You are with us.

Or

Call to Worship

One: We have come to worship, it is good to be here!
All: We are here with friends;
      we rejoice in "the ties that bind."
One: We have come to worship, it is good to be here!
All: We meet new people; we will share fresh experiences.
One: We have come to worship, it is good to be here!
All: We join together in prayer and praise;
      we hear the Word for us.

One: We have come to worship, it is good to be here!

All: **We renew our commitment to Jesus Christ;**
we seek to serve him faithfully.

Opening Prayer

One: Join with all those who praise our God.

All: **Join with the saints of all the ages.**

One: Join with Martin Luther, and Martin Luther King, and Mother Teresa.

All: **Join with family members who have gone from our sight, and are**
lovingly remembered.

One: Join with those who meet in this church this morning.

All: **Join with Christians of our town/city, and Christians in far corners**
of our world.

One: May the praise of all resound to the Glory of God.

All: **May our worship inspire us to work in the Way of Jesus Christ.**
Amen.

Prayer of Confession

One: You call us to commitment, O God.

All: **When apathy prevents us from beginning the task, inspire us.**

One: You call us to commitment, O God.

All: **When we find excuses for not carrying out the faithful task,**
alert us.

One: You call us to commitment, O God.

All: **When your priorities are clear but we ignore them, confront us.**

One: You call us to commitment, O God.

All: **When we see the need to work with others, enable us to make the**
first move.

One: You call us to commitment, O God.

All: **In the midst of hard struggle, set before us the example of Jesus**
Christ, who suffered yet won through.

   (Time for silent reflection)

Words of Assurance

One: O God, you enable us to reflect on those ingrained attitudes, that natural reluctance, those personality flaws, that fear of the unknown, and that lack of trust, which prevent us from being your faithful people.

All: **You give us a fresh willingness to act as followers of Jesus Christ.**

One: You are ready to revitalize your commitment.

All: **The peace of Jesus Christ is ours. Amen.**

Offering Prayer

One: Teach us the joy of sharing, O God:

All: **The joy of sharing time with those who lack friendship and care, the joy of sharing attention with those who are anxious and afraid, the joy of sharing gifts with those whom this world treats harshly.**

One: Bless these gifts as they work in the Way of Jesus.

All: **Amen.**

Commissioning

One: Discover the right path!

All: **We will walk resolutely along it.**

One: Sense the temptation to avoid and delay!

All: **We will fight that temptation.**

One: Be aware of the tendency to make excuses!

All: **We will counter it with enthusiasm.**

One: Realize the good work that can be accomplished with others!

All: **We will commit ourselves to the work.**

One: Remember the Christian name you bear!

All: **We will strive to be worthy of Jesus Christ.**

Sunday between
July 3 and 9 inclusive

Proper 9 [14]

2 Kings 5:1–14
Psalm 30
Galatians 6:(1–6), 7–16
Luke 10:1–11, 16–20

Call to Worship

One: Creator of calm,

All: Even with our uneasiness and fear, we approach you.

One: Promise of forgiveness,

All: Even though we are aware of our shortcomings, we come before you.

One: Giver of hope,

All: Even though we lack confidence for the journey, we approach you.

One: Source of compassion,

All: Even though we lack your healing spirit, we come before you. Let us worship God.

Opening Prayer

One: Breathe your creative spirit into us, O God,

All: That we may discover new ways to promote acceptance and compassion.

One: Breathe your supportive spirit into us, O God,

All: That we may bring courage to those who feel powerless.

One: Breathe your understanding spirit into us, O God,

All: That we may know how it feels to walk in another's shoes.

One: Breathe your loving spirit into us, O God,

All: That we may find joy as faithful followers of Jesus Christ. Amen.

Prayer of Confession *(for peace)*

One: We know the peace of summer when we are outdoors on a beautiful evening, among family or friends. But we seek your Shalom, O God, your deep peace.

All: **When we are tempted to avoid an essential decision, give us peace through taking action.**

One: When we are tempted to let needed words go unsaid, give us peace through speaking up.

All: **When we are tempted to remain stay-at-home disciples, give us peace through a missionary zeal.**

One: When we are tempted to leave the task of spreading the Good News to others, give us peace through confidently sharing the Gospel.

All: **When we are tempted to put our spiritual life into the background, give us peace through a renewed life of faith.**

One: When we are tempted to forget the needs of a suffering world, give us peace through sharing our gifts.

All: **When we are tempted to worship the gods of selfishness, and of superficial pleasure, give us peace as we offer praise and thankfulness to you, the living God.**

　　(Time for silent reflection)

Or

Prayer of Confession *(for awareness of ministry)*

One: You call us to many ministries, O God.
　　You call us to the ministry of compassion.

All: **When we fail to notice need, or when we turn away from need, forgive us!**

One: You call us to many ministries, O God.
　　You call us to a ministry of teaching.

All: **When we feel our learning days are over, or when we hold back from communicating a new way, forgive us!**

One: You call us to many ministries, O God.
　　You call us to a ministry of forgiveness.

All: **When we will not see another person's point of view, or when we cannot leave what is past in the past, forgive us!**

One: You call us to many ministries, O God.
You call us to the ministry of proclaiming the Good News.

All: **When we lack the courage to speak Christ's hopeful and loving message to our family and friends, forgive us!**
(Time for silent reflection)

Words of Assurance

One: May the peace of Christ – who knew conflict, the agony of decision making, envy, rejection, and the power of the full forces of evil ranged against him – may the peace of Jesus Christ, be for you, within you, behind you, and before you, now and always.

All: **Thanks be to God. Amen.**

Offering Prayer

One: Faithfully we come before you, O God,
joyfully acknowledging the gifts that we have received.

All: **Faithfully we share our gifts.**
They reflect our discipleship,
they influence our discipleship,
they encourage our discipleship,
and they will make a difference within this local church,
and in communities far from here,
through our mission funds. Amen.

Commissioning

One: Ready for action, we leave this service.

All: **We will reflect humbly.**
We will decide carefully.
We will go out confidently.
We will act resolutely.
We will grow steadily.
We will love wholeheartedly.

Sunday between
July 10 and 16 inclusive

Proper 10 [15]

Amos 7:7–17
Psalm 82
Colossians 1:1–14
Luke 10:25–37

Call to Worship

One: From the Swiss Alps, from New York City, from the shores of Lake
Superior, *(substitute other locations as appropriate in current news),*
All: **God's people are called to worship.**
One: In French and English, in Swahili and Spanish,
All: **God's people rejoice in worship.**
One: In moments of celebration, at times of loss;
for the sacrament of Baptism, around the Lord's table,
All: **God's people are joined for worship.**
One: With the love of God in their hearts; ready to risk and learn,
All: **God's people find fulfillment in worship.**
One: Let us then, the spiritual descendants of Knox and Wesley, Luther and
Cranmer, wholeheartedly worship God. *(Substitute names of other
church leaders if appropriate.)*

Opening Prayer

One: Giving thanks for your wonderful gifts in creation, O God,
All: **Is our worship privilege.**
One: Raising our voices in glorious praise, O God,
All: **Is our heartfelt worship response.**
One: Hearing your Word of challenge, and being inspired to act, O God,
All: **Is our worship opportunity.**
One: Your love for us in Jesus Christ, your Cherished One, and your eternal
Way, O God,
All: **Is the source and focus of our joy in worship. Amen.**

Prayer of Confession

One: When we sense we are habit bound, or stuck in the old routine,

All: Give us the courage, O God, to break with the past.

One: When we sense we have talents to share, or support to offer,

All: Give us the confidence, O God, to risk the new and untried ways.

One: When we sense that there are friendships to foster, hurts to bring out into the open,

All: Give us the assurance, O God, that relationships will be renewed.

One: When we sense that our faith is weak, our Christian confidence low,

All: Give us your Spirit, O God, that we may rejoice in our living, speak up for the truth, and act decisively with the needy ones.

(Time for silent reflection)

Words of Assurance

One: You stir us from apathy and complacency, O God.
You give us a vision which can transform our living and the life of this faith community, and we rejoice.

All: We are ready to venture out on a new path, the path of renewed Christian endeavor, the path that leads to God's peace.

One: God's support and peace are yours.

All: Thanks be to God. Amen.

Or

Prayer of Confession *(about neighbors)*

One: Have we thought, "Who are our neighbors?"

All: They are the family members and friends we know. We love them, we listen to them, we argue with them.

One: Who are our neighbors?

All: They are the members and friends of our faith community. We worship with them, we work with them, we disagree with them.

One: Who are our neighbors?

All: They live in our locality. We chat with them, we share news with them, we have common problems, and enjoy a joke with them.

One: Who are our neighbors?

All: **They live far from our home and church; we do not know their names. We support them with our gifts, we speak and act with them for freedom, out of a living standard we take for granted.**

One: Jesus reminds us that there is a measure of neighborliness. "Love your neighbor as you love yourself."

All: **How do we measure up?**

    (Time for silent reflection)

Words of Assurance

One: We will take our responsibility to our neighbors seriously.

All: **The ones we love, the ones we like, the ones we don't get along with.**

One: As you make the "Golden Rule" your own, wonderful things happen, surprising changes take place.

All: **Quarrels are forgotten, prejudices are overcome, sharing is second nature.**

One: And God's peace is yours, the peace that lasts.

All: **Thanks be to God. Amen.**

Offering Prayer

One: These gifts will be blessed as we help our neighbors,

All: **Our downhearted faith community neighbors,**

One: Our suffering city/rural neighbors,

All: **Our needy church neighbors throughout this nation,**

One: And our global neighbors facing persecution and hardship.

All: **We know, O God, that you will bless the work that these gifts make possible. Amen.**

Or

Offering Prayer

One: You will not leave us stranded beside the highway, O God.

All: **You will pick us up and take us to shelter, and attend to our wounds.**

One: With these gifts we have the power to be "Good Samaritans" for our church, and for many far from this place.

All: **Bless these gifts, that they may be used**
as Jesus would have them used,
compassionately, without discrimination, and generously. Amen.

Commissioning

One: You lead us out to serve, O God.

All: **Give us courage to help the disadvantaged.**

One: Give us the willingness to offer a second chance.

All: **Give us patience when trouble comes.**

One: Give us wisdom when choices must be made.

All: **Give us peace in the midst of turmoil.**

One: Give us your graceful presence when all else fails.

Or

Commissioning

One: You are your brother's keeper;

All: **We will pay attention to the needs of our loved ones.**

One: You are your neighbor's keeper;

All: **We will serve those who live near to us.**

One: You are a keeper of your faith community;

All: **We will play an active part in the support of this church.**

One: You are a keeper of the needy stranger;

All: **We will find out what we can do, to help the abused and power-less, far from this city/town/village.**

Sunday between
July 17 and 23 inclusive

Proper 11[16]

Amos 8:1–12
Psalm 52
Colossians 1:15–28
Luke 10:38–42

Call to Worship

One: The warming rays of the summer sun,

All: Reflect the warmth of God's love for us.

One: The crops growing; strengthening and maturing,

All: Reflect our growth in faith from one season of life to the next.

One: The cool rippling water of the lake, the gently flowing stream,
(*substitute other landscape features as appropriate*),

All: Reflect for us God's cleansing and renewing power.

One: The laughter of families and friends gathered to enjoy food and
friendship in the open air,

**All: Reflect the joy and thankfulness of God's own people gathering
together for worship. Let us worship God!**

Opening Prayer

One: You call practical persons to worship, O God:

**All: The cooks and cleaners, those who work with hammers, and those
who wield paintbrushes.**

One: You call the counselors and advisors to worship, O God:

**All: The social workers and teachers, those who work with feelings and
those who work with computers.**

One: You call retired women and men to worship, O God:

**All: The fit and the struggling, those who enjoy gardening, those who
care for their grandchildren.**

One: You call boys and girls to worship, O God:

All: The shy ones and the daring, those who enjoy soccer, those who play baseball.

One: You call the challenged ones to worship, O God:

All: Persons of varied abilities, those who wheel happily, and those who sign joyfully.

One: You call us *all* to worship, O God:

All: We rejoice in this wonderful opportunity! Amen.

Prayer of Confession

One: When we have been so caught up with achieving and doing, that we forget to take time to be quiet,

All: God of the still small voice, forgive us.

One: When we have been so focused on reflecting and meditating that we forget to practice compassion and helping,

All: God of Jesus, the healer and teacher, forgive us.

One: When we are so concerned to speak out for the powerless that we forget our nearest and dearest,

All: God who has placed us in families, forgive us.

One: When we are so concerned for those who are our loved ones and friends that we forget the despised and rejected,

All: God who stands beside the exploited and abused, forgive us.
   (Time for silent reflection)

Words of Assurance

One: Help us, O God, to stand back from the routine happenings of our lives, and to reflect on them your loving light.

All: You will show us clearly, when we should talk
and when we should act.
You will show us clearly what changes need to be made,
which relationships need to be renewed,
and which situations call us to begin again.

One: In calm reflection and in fresh starts, pardon and peace will be yours!

All: Thanks be to God! Amen.

Offering Prayer

One: Unfailing are your blessings to us, O God, unfailingly appropriate and generous.

All: **In response to your unfailing generosity to us, we bring our gifts for blessing.**

One: We will be blessed in this church, as gifts are transformed into teaching, listening, and singing.

All: **In the wider church, our gifts will be transformed into healthier communities, training for jobs, and lively centers of faith. Amen.**

Commissioning

One: Ever with us in past days, O God, you are with us still.

All: **You are with us as we reflect on the modern-day saints in action.**

One: You are with us as we pose the hard questions and are challenged by the answers.

All: **You are with us as we struggle to work out life's direction with Christ as a pattern.**

One: You are with us as we venture fearfully into new territory.

All: **You are with us as we leave this church to faithfully begin a new week.**

One: O loving, joyful, and careful God,

All: **Thank you! Amen.**

Sunday between
July 24 and 30 inclusive

Proper 12 [17]

Hosea 1:2–10
Psalm 85
Colossians 2:6–15, (16–19)
Luke 11:1–13

Call to Worship

One: From our homes you call us to prayer, O God.
All: We pray for all who make our homes good places to be.
One: To our faith community you call us in prayer, O God.
All: We pray for all our friends who worship and serve Jesus.
One: With our needs and anxieties you call us to prayer, O God.
All: We pray you will have a Word for us.
One: As disciples of Jesus you call us to prayer, O God.
All: We pray that his faithful prayer life will be ours.

Or

Call to Worship

One: We turn from the anxieties and the challenges of our own situation, O God – decisions to be taken, worries over health, and the concern for loved ones,
All: To be open to a renewed life, with your love at the center of it.
One: We turn from the Sunday pleasures and pastimes, O God, of shopping and fishing, camping and playing baseball,
All: To seek a time of spiritual refreshment in prayer and praise, a time to bring our thanksgiving to you.
One: We turn, O God, from a society where money rules, and the powerless are ignored,
All: To knock on the door that opens to justice and acceptance, the door that leads to your glorious Realm.

Opening Prayer

One: Joyfully we come before you, O God.

**All: We celebrate the life you have given us,
and our ability to enjoy it.**

One: Thankfully we come before you, O God.

**All: We have received so much, so often,
and our thanks overflows.**

One: Conscious of our faults, we come before you, O God.

**All: We are aware of your willingness to forgive,
and to grant us a fresh start.**

One: Prayerfully we come before you, O God,

**All: For in prayer you engage us,
and open up the way ahead. Amen.**

Prayer of Confession

One: Like a good friend you are there for us, O God,
making us laugh, celebrating the moment.

All: You encourage us to enjoy life to the fullest.

One: Like a good friend, you are there for us, O God,
knowing us so well, utterly to be trusted.

All: You encourage us to deepen friendship.

One: Like a good friend, you are there for us, O God,
listening so carefully, yet slow to judge.

All: You encourage us to listen with empathy.

One: Like a good friend, you are there for us, O God,
ready to point out our talents, before our shortcomings.

All: You encourage us to look for the best in others.

One: Like a good friend, you are there for us, O God,
challenging us to share our gifts with others.

All: You encourage us to participate in community.
(Time for silent reflection)

Or

Prayer of Confession *(reflecting on the Lord's Prayer)*

One: "Our Father...hallowed be thy name..."

All: **Your name, O God, is the Holy Name,**
but we confess that we make holy some unholy names,
and worship other gods.

One: "Thy Kingdom come..."

All: **We long for your glorious reign, O God,**
but we confess that we fail to advance the just sharing
and the compassionate attitudes, which are signs of your rule.

One: "Give us this day our daily bread..."

All: **You provide so graciously for us, O God,**
but we confess that the needs of so many,
for the basic necessities of life, fail to move us.

One: "Forgive us our trespasses, as we forgive those who trespass against us..."

All: **We find forgiving those who have hurt us,**
hard work, O God,
but we confess that our difficulty is rooted in our inability to
forgive ourselves.

One: "And lead us not into temptation, but deliver us from evil…"

All: **Sometimes, we confess, we go willingly into temptation,**
sometimes we fail to listen to our consciences
and to those who love us best.
(Time for silent reflection)

Words of Assurance

One: Gently, and with good humor, O God, you show us the realities of our
personality, and of our situation.

All: **You show us that change is possible,**
and encourage us to make changes that will be good for us,
and for those around us.

One: In reflection, realization, and action, peace will come!

All: **Thanks be to God! Amen.**

Offering Prayer

One: You are the source of change for good, Living God.

All: **Through these gifts, you bring help to the distressed;**
through our prayers, you bring hope alive;
through our words and actions, you encourage the suffering and
oppressed.
Bless us, bless our gifts, as your love goes to work. Amen.

Commissioning

One: An end to apathy and a beginning of confidence –

All: **Your wish is our command, O God.**

One: An end to avoiding responsibility, a beginning to face reality –

All: **Your wish is our command, O God.**

One: An end to religion as a burden, a beginning to joy in the Gospel Way –

All: **Your wish is our command, O God.**

One: An end to the cares that bewilder us, a beginning to your loving
accepting presence –

All: **Your wish is our command, O God.**

Or

Commissioning

One: We pray as we leave this church.
We pray for your presence, God,

All: **When others are not there for us.**

One: We pray for your assurance, God,

All: **When our confidence fails us.**

One: We pray for your Realm, God,

All: **When political leaders keep it at a distance.**

One: We pray for your peace, God,

All: **When bitterness and conflict are the order of the day.**

One: We pray for your Spirit, God,

All: **When the gods of this world lead us astray.**

Sunday between
July 31 and August 6 inclusive

Proper 13 [18]

Hosea 11:1–11
Psalm 107:1–9, 43
Colossians 3:1–11
Luke 12:13–21

Call to Worship

One: Give thanks to God, because God is good.

All: God's love has no limits.

One: Some people were as lost as travelers without a map.

All: Some people lacked food, water, or a roof over their heads.

One: In their distress they called out to God for help.

All: God put them on the right road. God met their most basic needs.

One: God worked through compassionate and faithful men and women.

All: This is God's nature, to help people who are going through hard times.

One: Let us praise and thank God, for God's constant love.

Opening Prayer

All: We come, Loving God, as searchers for the truth about you.

One: We look for the source of your creative genius.

**All: We marvel at the delicate spider's web;
we are amazed at the power of the hummingbird;
we wonder at the growth of the sunflower.**

One: We look for the source of your inspired presence among men and women.

**All: We marvel at those whose lives are an imitation of Jesus;
we wonder at faith communities who bring justice and healing in Christlike ways,
we are amazed that Christians are still ready to sacrifice for the poorest and least powerful.**

Our looking is perceiving,
Our seeking is finding,
Our uncertainty is faithfulness.
We will not cease from the search, Loving and Ever-Present God.
Amen.

Prayer of Confession

One: Getting, saving, hoarding –

All: We confess, O God, our tendency to keep our material possessions to ourselves.

One: Getting, saving, hoarding –

All: We confess, O God, our tendency to hang back from affirming and encouraging those close to us.

One: Getting, saving, hoarding –

All: We confess, O God, that we are aware of crying needs in our community, but we are reluctant to share from our resources of time, ability, and money.

One: Getting, saving, hoarding –

All: We confess, O God, we are aware of huge inequalities in our world, but we are reluctant to support and give for those we do not know.

One: Jesus reminds us that life does not last forever.
       (Time for silent reflection)

Words of Assurance

One: God, you will give us a generous spirit,
       you will open us up to new ways of sharing and advocacy.

**All: We will open our minds to new truth, and ways of sharing that truth;
we will open our hearts to the needs around us;
we will share our money with the powerless, the poor, and the suffering.**

One: This is the way to know the peace of God.

All: Thanks be to God! Amen.

Offering Prayer

One: Loving God, you call us to venture, to risk, and to join with others on our Christian adventure.

All: **Bless these gifts, that persons we know well**
and persons whose names we will never know,
will be empowered to bring healing,
challenge, and compassion to many. Amen.

Commissioning

One: May generosity be your watchword!

All: **We will share from our plenty.**
We will give for the needy.
We will praise lavishly.
We will encourage frequently.
We will care passionately.
We will love wholeheartedly.

One: And the God whose generosity was shown in Jesus Christ will go with you!

Sunday between
August 7 and 13 inclusive
Proper 14 [19]

Isaiah 1:1, 10–20
Psalm 50:1–8, 22–23
Hebrews 11:1–3, 8–16
Luke 12:32–40

Call to Worship
One: We come into your presence, O God, a community of faith, proud of our venturing heritage.

All: **Abraham set out with Sarah and found a new land.**

One: Moses went into the desert, to escape the persecution of Pharaoh.

All: **Nehemiah returned to Jerusalem, and re-established a worshipping community.**

One: Jesus returned to Jerusalem and overcame the forces of evil.

All: **In the confidence of our faith tradition, let us worship God!**

Opening Prayer
One: All power is yours, Almighty God,

All: **Creator of mountains, origin of life, source of countless galaxies.**

One: All good is yours, Compassionate God,

All: **Inspiration of the caregivers, sustainer of the powerless, motivator of the justice seekers.**

One: All hopefulness is yours, Eternal God,

All: **Encourager of the downhearted, light in the dark places, defeater of death.**

One: All love is yours, Anointer of Jesus,

All: **Bond of faith community, life-giver to the saints, value-bringer to our troubled planet.**
   We praise you world without end. Amen.

Prayer of Confession

One: When we hang back from saying the words which are on our hearts;
 words of comfort,
 words of challenge,
 words to bring peace,

All: O God, give us the readiness to speak out.
 (Time for silent reflection)

One: When we are conscious of deeply troubling feelings;
 anger towards a person,
 guilt over a past wrong,
 bitterness stemming from a chance event in life,

All: O God, give us the readiness to openly express our feelings.
 (Time for silent reflection)

One: When we see the needy ones around us;
 lacking a supportive family,
 lacking life's basic necessities,
 lacking the love of a friend,

All: O God, give us the readiness to act.
 (Time for silent reflection)

Words of Assurance

One: O God, you alert us, and you bring us confidence,

All: You enable us to say the words that need saying,
 You enable us to take the actions which need to be taken.
 We rejoice in your strong presence, for the good times,
 and for the challenging times.

One: Pardon and peace are yours.

All: Thanks be to God! Amen.

Offering Prayer

One: We do not meet all the people that our gifts reach,
       we cannot feel their pain or know their struggle.

All: **But we give with generous hearts; and we give in faith,**
      for we know that you, Loving God,
      will bless the compassion, the freedom, and the community
      that these gifts make possible. Amen.

Commissioning

One: You are a people ready for adventure!

All: **We venture forth to risk life-giving experiences.**
      We venture forth to challenge clear evidence of injustice.
      We venture forth to meet the needs of troubled loved ones.
      We venture forth with Christ's example before us.
      We venture forth with God's peace to secure us.

Sunday between
August 14 and 20 inclusive

Proper 15 [20]

Isaiah 5:1–7
Psalm 80:1–2, 8–19
Hebrews 11:29 – 12:2
Luke 12:49–56

Call to Worship *(adapted from Hebrews 11:29 – 12:2)*

One: Faithfulness is the mark of your people, O God,

All: The faith of Rahab, the faith of David, the faith of Samuel, the faith of the prophets.

One: The faithful ones in times past blessed your name, O God, and worked in your way.

All: It cost them persecution and torture; for some it cost their lives.

One: We remember what faithfulness cost Jesus – abuse and a cross.

All: And now we are called to be faithful,

One: To run with determination the race that is before us,

All: Keeping our eyes fixed on Jesus as we do so.

One: It will not be easy, but you, O God,
will deal gracefully with us.

All: Thanks be to you, O God!

Opening Prayer

One: For the warmth of the sun, the beauty of the lake,

All: We bring our praise to you, Creator God.

One: For the inspiration of worship,

All: We bring our praise to you, Holy God.

One: For the joy in fellowship, the support of friends,

All: We bring our praise to you, God of the Church.

One: For the need that comes home to us, the challenge to serve,

All: We bring our praise to you, merciful God.
        God of our world, God of our church.
        God ever present to each one of us,
        we praise you. Amen.

Prayer of Affirmation

One: You are with us in the testing times, O God.
All: **When good health deserts us, when depression clouds us,
        you are there.**
One: You are with us in the testing times, O God.
All: **When friendships sour, and loved ones turn away,
        you are there.**
One: You are with us in the testing times, O God.
All: **When doubts challenge us, when faith will not sustain us,
        you are there.**
One: You are with us in the testing times, O God.
All: **When our dreams are shattered,
        when our limited lifespan comes home to us,
        you are there.**
One: You are with us in the testing times, O God.
All: **When terror and war disturb us, come home to us,
        you are there.**
One: The presence of peace, the inspiration to bring change, source of
        eternal hope, you are there.
            (Time for silent reflection)

Words of Assurance

One: Ever-Loving God, you give us the hope that renewal will happen,
All: **That life will be enjoyed fully again,
        that friendships will be restored again,
        that faith will come alive again,
        that dreams will inspire us again,
        that war and terror will cease.**
One: God's peace is for you!
All: **Thanks be to God! Amen.**

Offering Prayer

One: The gifts you bless, O God, enable each one of us to grow.
The gifts you bless, O God, enable us to support each other.
The gifts you bless, O God, enable our faith community to grow.
The gifts you bless, O God, enable the global church to grow.

All: **You bless them as we are encouraged,**
you bless them as friendship deepens,
you bless them as our faith roots are nourished by your Word,
you bless them as we share with persons whose names we will never
know.

One: Your blessing goes with us on our Christian journey.

All: **And your people, O God, reflect this blessing. Amen.**

Commissioning

One: May the Spirit of God, into our minutes and days, breathe purpose.

All: **May the Spirit of God, into our families and relationships, breathe**
faithfulness.

One: May the Spirit of God, into our church, breathe commitment to the
Living Way,

All: **Through all, enfolding all, permeating all, may the Spirit of God**
breathe love.

Sunday between
August 21 and 27 inclusive

Proper 16 [21]

Jeremiah 1:4–10
Psalm 71:1–6
Hebrews 12:18–29
Luke 13:10–17

Call to Worship *(based on Jeremiah 1)*

One: O God, you knew us before we were born.

All: **Throughout our life you have gone with us.**

One: You know our reluctance to speak and work for you.

All: **But you say, "Believe in yourselves you can do it!"**

One: We have no reason to fear, no reason to hang back.

All: **God will give us the words to say and the confidence to carry out our faithful tasks.**

Opening Prayer

One: You are our rock, O God, our strong foundation.

All: **We build our lives on your words of truth;**
the witness of your saints directs us.

One: You are our rock, O God, our strong foundation.

All: **We find a place in your family of faith;**
their friendship encourages us.

One: You are our rock, O God, our strong foundation.

All: **We are challenged to change our neighborhood for good,**
to bring healing and support to those around us.

One: You are our rock, O God, our strong foundation.

All: **We are confronted with darkness in our world;**
working in the light of Christ we can make a difference. Amen.

Prayer of Confession

One: Only you know how we are held back, O God.

All: Held back by self-doubts, held back by fear of the unknown.

One: Only you know our lack of freedom, O God.

All: Our reluctance to speak our mind, our unwillingness to think differently than our friends.

One: Only you know our most cherished dreams, O God.

All: Our desire to break free from the familiar way, to be liberated from the path that is mapped out for us.

One: Only you know our longing for joy in the spirit, O God.

All: Our need to experience your inspiring love, our will to straighten up all that is crooked in our part of this world.

(Time for silent reflection)

Words of Assurance

One: You cut us loose, O God; you let us feel our freedom, and choose our own way.

All: And if that way is faithful and fulfilling, you walk with us, sustaining us, and supporting us.

One: The freely chosen way is the way
that leads to peace of body, mind, and spirit.

All: We will accept that peace, thanks be to God! Amen.

Offering

One: You free us to offer the best we are able, O God.

All: The best of our gifts.
The best of our striving.
The best of our friendship.
The best of our faithfulness.
The best of our abilities.
The best of our will for justice.
The best of our eternal hopefulness.

One: Nothing is offered to God in vain!

All: God will receive our offerings and richly bless them. Amen.

Commissioning

One: From here to the waiting world is just a few steps.
We leave this sanctuary with confidence.

All: **God will enable us to make the crooked paths straight,**
and the rough places smooth.
God will grant us freedom from the ways that restrict us,
and boundless joy in our adventuring.
God will give us love within our families,
and trust within our deepest friendships.
And God will never leave us in this earthly time,
or when this time merges with eternity.

One: Go in peace, you are ready for the journey!

Sunday between
August 28 and September 3 inclusive

Proper 17 [22]

Jeremiah 2:4–13
Psalm 81:1, 10–16
Hebrews 13:1–8, 15–16
Luke 14:1, 7–14

Call to Worship

One: Rejoice in the community of Jesus Christ!

All: We have gathered together for praise and thanksgiving.

One: Rejoice in the community of Jesus Christ!

(If celebrating Baptism/Confirmation or equivalent)

All: We have gathered together to celebrate the entry of young persons into the church.

(Otherwise)

All: We have gathered to celebrate our common tradition.

One: Rejoice in the community of Jesus Christ!

All: We have gathered to hear the Good News!

One: Rejoice in the community of Jesus Christ!

**All: We will commit ourselves to the Way of Jesus Christ;
to justice and acceptance,
to reconciliation and caregiving.
Let us worship God!**

Opening Prayer

One: You meet us, O God, at every place along the highway of life.

All: You meet us at life's beginning – smiling, gurgling, and vulnerable.

One: You meet us as children, growing and exploring, yet laughing and teasing as we go.

All: You meet us as young adults, finding our feet, maturing and searching for values.

One: You meet us as parents, with all the responsibility, joy, and frustration that comes with parenthood.

All: **You meet us in the autumn of our days, with wisdom, yet with increasing infirmity.**

One: You meet us, O God, at every stage in life, for you are a trusted and sustaining presence.

All: **Yet we know you remain always ahead of us – the source of hope and the essence of eternity.**
Praise be to your name, Living God, Parent of Jesus! Amen.

Prayer of Confession *(for humility)*

One: We aim to carve out a reputation, to find a place of honor in the world.

All: **Help us to serve consistently and compassionately in the Christian way; humble us, O God.**

One: We aim to listen carefully to our friends and family members, but we talk about ourselves.

All: **Help us to concentrate on the other person; humble us, O God.**

One: We aim to enthusiastically support the community of Jesus Christ, but other priorities get in the way.

All: **Help us to see and understand the need for Christian values; humble us, O God.**

One: We aim to speak out against poverty and injustice, but our lifestyle betrays the words we say.

All: **Give us the courage to practice justice and simplicity; humble us, O God.**

One: We aim to grow as disciples of Jesus, but it is more comfortable to stay with the tried and tested realities.

All: **Help us to go through the process of questioning and doubt; humble us, O God.**
(Time for silent reflection)

Words of Assurance

One: You call us to account, O God, for pride and self-interest are ours.

All: **We will reflect on the needs of the powerless and disadvantaged, rather than our own.**
We will reflect on how we can serve, rather than how much we can get.
We will hear another out, before we offer an opinion.
We will judge slowly, and forgive generously.

One: Humility led Jesus all the way to a cross. It is not an easy way for you.

All: **It is the way of peace for us.**

One: Thanks be to God!

All: **Amen.**

Offering Prayer

One: Beyond our realized talents and abilities,

All: **You call us to act.**

One: Way beyond our boundaries of community,

All: **You call us to serve.**

One: Beyond our conventional understanding of stewardship,

All: **You call us to give.**

One: Bless all our gifts,

All: **In the name of your supreme gift, Jesus. Amen.**

Commissioning

One: When we are tempted to overvalue our self-importance,

All: **Lift our eyes to the starry sky.**

One: When we think we have all the answers,

All: **Let a child come and ask us questions.**

One: When our friends and family flatter us,

All: **Ask how we respond to the poorest and least able.**

Sunday between
September 4 and 10 inclusive

Proper 18 [23]

Jeremiah 18:1–11
Psalm 139:1–6, 13–18
Philemon 1–21
Luke 14:25–33

Call to Worship

One: The voice of God is heard in all the world.
All: **In troubled lands, where people hunger and fear, it speaks of compassionate action.**
One: The voice of God is heard in the church.
All: **In encouragement of each other, in support of wider church, it speaks of community.**
One: The voice of God is heard within each one of us.
All: **It speaks of acceptance, it speaks of forgiveness, it speaks of peace, it speaks of hope.**
One: It speaks now; it will never be silent!
All: **Let us listen to God's voice.**

Or

Call to Worship *(based on Psalm 139)*

One: You know us so well, O God!
All: **Working or resting, praising or praying, it's nothing new to you.**
One: You know us so well, O God!
All: **Ahead of us and behind us, you are with us all our life.**
One: You know us so well, O God!
All: **Creator of us and our world, inspiration of all our days.**
One: You know us so well, O God!
All: **Beyond our understanding, yet for us and with us, all the time.**

Opening Prayer

One: You have blessed us with the sunlit glory of summer days.

Choir: And we praise you, Creator God.

One: You have blessed us with a Christian community of friends.

All: And we rejoice in our mutual support, O God.

One: You have blessed us with questioning, enthusiastic young persons, and with older persons full of good sense.

Men and Boys: Together they are our strength, O God.

One: You have blessed us with a church which stands with the powerless.

Women and Girls: And we know it reflects your mercy and compassion, O Loving God.

One: You have blessed us with the Way of Jesus.

All: And we will strive to make the Way of Jesus shine through all our venturing together, and through the path which we tread alone, eternal and ever present God. Amen.

Prayer of Confession

One: To build a community of disciples, we must be ready to appreciate the gifts and talents of some very different persons.

All: When we are not prepared to search carefully for the hidden abilities of others, perceptive God, forgive us!

One: To build a community of disciples, we must be ready to listen to the deepest concerns of our friends in Christ.

All: When we fail to listen with our heart as well as with mind, compassionate God, forgive us!

One: To build a community of disciples, we must be ready to walk the gospel walk, as well as talk the gospel talk.

All: When commitment is hard and selfish priorities win the day, suffering God, forgive us!

One: To build a community of disciples, we must be ready to listen to new truth and act courageously on what we hear.

All: When our minds are closed, and our hearts remain unmoved by the needs of the tested ones, God of continuing revelation, forgive us!

One: To build a community of disciples, we must be ready to place Jesus Christ at the center of our life's pattern.

All: When we deny the cost of following Jesus Christ and ignore the challenge of his teaching, Loving God, forgive us!
(Time for silent reflection)

Words of Assurance

One: New life is your gift.

All: **In the discovery of new insights,**
in the acceptance of new truths,
in the naming of evil persons and evil work,
in the refusal to let guilt overburden us,
in the willingness to work to joyfully with fellow Christians,
in the reality of discipleship's cost,
new life is ours, abundant life is possible.

One: Sin is overcome; pardon and peace are truly yours!

All: **Thanks be to God! Amen.**

Offering Prayer

One: Given freely, may these gifts bring freedom

All: **To the powerless and rejected,**
to the questioning and the sad,
to the distressed and anxious,
in the freeing Spirit of Jesus Christ. Amen.

Commissioning

One: We respond to God as we leave the church.
Having heard your Word, O God, encourage us to reflect and act.

All: **Having seen the signs, give us confidence to follow.**

One: Having sensed the truth, help us to be faithful.

All: **Having encountered Jesus, lead us to discipleship.**

Sunday between
September 11 and 17 inclusive

Proper 19 [24]

Jeremiah 4:11–12, 22–28
Psalm 14
1 Timothy 1:12–17
Luke 15:1–10

Call to Worship

One: Give thanks to God for this morning.

All: The glory of God's creation is spread before us.

One: Give thanks to God for our living.

All: The love of family and friends surrounds us.

One: Give thanks to God for this hour of worship.

All: The opportunity to praise and pray, to listen and reflect, is grace to us. Let us worship God!

Or

Call to Worship

One: God, who cares for us as a shepherd cares for the flock,

All: Calls us to worship.

One: God, who loves us as a mother loves her baby,

All: Is here for us as we worship.

One: God, whose love for us exceeds the depth of our understanding,

All: Is heartfelt joy to us as we worship.

One: God, who challenges us to feel the world's pain and bring healing,

All: Is inspiration to us as we worship.

One: God, whose community of faith goes beyond all space and time,

All: Is eternal hope to us as we worship.

Opening Prayer

One: Come join our celebration, Loving God!

All: We are gathered as a faith community of prayer and praise.

One: Come join our celebration, Loving God!

All: We give thanks for your creative, life-giving presence.

One: Come join our celebration, Loving God!

All: Your Word is inspiration, and light in the dark places.

One: Come join our celebration, Loving God!

All: To know you is a joy, and to faithfully serve you is a delight. Amen.

(Alternate last response, if celebrating baptism)

For your joy is our joy, as this family of faith is renewed at the waters of baptism. Amen.

Or

Opening Prayer for Covenanting at the Start of Church School

One: We are a celebrating community, Loving God.

All: We celebrate the faithfulness of all who worship, Sunday by Sunday.

One: We are a celebrating community, Loving God.

All: We celebrate the joy of young persons returning to church school, and the dedication of their teachers.

One: We are a celebrating community, Loving God.

All: We celebrate the prophets, leaders, and heroes of the Hebrew Scriptures, and the New Covenant revealed in Jesus Christ.

One: We are a celebrating community, Loving God.

All: We celebrate the work of your Holy Spirit, bringing compassion, justice, and a challenge to each of us, and to this church. Amen.

Prayer of Confession

One: You are the seeker after the lost, O God.

You put us on the right path when we have gone astray.

In the rush of daily living, we have lost the ability to be still.

All: You find us, O God, in a willingness to seek moments of peace amidst the busiest days.

One: In our haste to judge others harshly, we have lost the ability to see the good in each person.

All: **You find us, O God, as we look compassionately and discover skills and values of lasting worth.**

One: In our pursuit of personal gain, we have lost the ability to meet the needs of the downhearted and the despised.

All: **You find us, O God, as we encourage the distressed and share our resources with those whose needs are great.**

One: In our concern to be successful in this world, we have lost the way of faith which leads to your Realm.

All: **You find us, O God, in a return to Christian discipleship, and a sharing with others in Christ's life-bringing work.**

Words of Assurance

One: As a shepherd ventures forth to find the one lost sheep,
so you go out, O Loving God, to bring us home.

All: **As we recognize our failings,**
and dedicate ourselves to your liberating Way;
as we follow your Way with confidence,
so peace is ours, and new life opens up for us.

One: Know release from your sins, and the freedom of Jesus Christ!

All: **Thanks be to God. Amen.**

Offering Prayer

One: O God, your generous provision for us goes way beyond the limits.

All: **May we give as you give:**
to foster compassion,
to enlighten through teaching,
to encourage talent,
to empower the rejected,
to fire up the dejected
to follow the Way of Jesus,
and to proclaim his saving grace to the lost. Amen.

Commissioning

One: The lost will be found!

All: We will search with commitment.
We will put them on the right path.
We will place God's choices before them.
We will enable forgiveness to be accepted.
We will be the bearers of compassion.
We will acknowledge our presence among the lost.

One: The lost will be found! We will be found!

All: And we will celebrate!

Sunday between
September 18 and 24 inclusive

Proper 20 [25]

Jeremiah 8:18 – 9:1
Psalm 79:1–9
1 Timothy 2:1–7
Luke 16:1–13

Call to Worship

One: Gather with Abraham and Moses, with Isaiah and Jeremiah.

All: **Remember that God has chosen a people for worship and service.**

One: Gather with Peter and James, with Stephen and Paul.

All: **Remember that God is with the followers of Jesus Christ.**

One: Gather with Francis and Augustine, with Martin Luther and Dietrich
Bonhoeffer.

All: **Remember that God has been faithful throughout the ages.**

One: Gather with local churches, and churches of this denomination
throughout the country;
gather with your fellow members of the worldwide church.

All: **Remember that God is with us, and the Good News of Jesus is ours
to share.**

Opening Prayer

One: Faithful in everything,

All: **You call us, O God, to the joy of worship, Sunday by Sunday.**

One: Faithful in everything,

All: **You call us, O God, to friendships which are healthy and sustaining.**

One: Faithful in everything,

All: **You call us, O God, to use our own resources compassionately and
justly.**

One: Faithful in everything,

All: **You call us, O God, to build up this faith community,
with kindness and with the values of Jesus Christ. Amen.**

A Prayer of Hope for Children

One: Our hope is that children will grow up nurtured by loving parents.

All: **Help us in our relationships of family and friendship to foster an atmosphere of love and security.**

One: Our hope is that children will be free to develop their own gifts and talents.

All: **Give us, O God, the willingness to see the special abilities of others; we will encourage them to put their talents to work.**

One: Our hope is that children will inherit a world where water is pure, where birdsong is heard, and where the earth is fertile.

All: **Enable us, O God, to hand over this planet to our children and grandchildren, in a more healthy state than in our day and generation.**

One: Our hope is that children will find joy and a sense of purpose through faith in Jesus Christ.

All: **Inspire us to persist on our faith journey, so that our quality of living may model the compassion and creativity that we wish for our children.**

One: Our hope is that children will find joy in their membership of the church.

All: **Encourage us, O God, to create an accepting fellowship where young and old learn from, and share with, one another.**

(Time for silent reflection)

Words of Assurance

One: Our hope is firmly in you, O God.

All: **We confess our lack of hope and our lack of trust in your loving power, so you will meet us, renew us, and set us on the path of faithfulness again.**

One: Feel the powerful, loving presence of God with you, granting you pardon and peace.

All: **We are aware of God's powerful love with us. Thanks be to God! Amen.**

Or

Prayer of Confession

One: You call us to use our opportunities, O God.

All: **When we have the chance to bring family or friends together, may we take it.**

One: You call us to use our opportunities, O God.

All: **When we have a chance to support and encourage others, may we do it.**

One: You call us to use our opportunities, O God.

All: **When we see a chance to volunteer in our faith or local community, may we be ready.**

One: You call us to use our opportunities, O God.

All: **When we see the chance to give, or to speak out for the downtrodden of our world, may we seize the moment.**

(Time for silent reflection)

Words of Assurance

One: It is so easy to hang back, to procrastinate. It is so easy to find reasons not to act. But God calls us to be alert, to be prepared, to be courageous.

All: **We will have our eyes open for the faithful opportunities; we will be ready to take them.**

One: God will bless your endeavors!

All: **And God's peace will be ours. Amen.**

Prayer of Dedication

One: Loving God, you will turn these gifts into smiling faces, new endeavors, words of comfort, moments of reflection, and laughing children.

All: **You will enable these gifts to go to work among the downtown homeless,**
and among the distressed in distant lands, whose names we will never know.

One: You can make these gifts a blessing to so many, and for this we thank you. Amen.

Commissioning

One: Use well what God has given you.

All: **We will use our prayers to discern the purpose of God,**
we will use the Bible to see God at work,
we will use the church to support and encourage us,
we will use our talents to serve others,
we will use the example of the saints to inspire us,
we will use the life and death of Jesus to guide us.

One: God will go with you! God is before you!

Sunday between
September 25 and October 1 inclusive

Proper 21 [26]

Jeremiah 32:1–3a, 6–15
Psalm 91:1–6, 14–16
1 Timothy 6:6–19
Luke 16:19–31

Call to Worship

One: Living God, you are the source of our security;
All: **In the midst of our troubles, you will be with us.**
One: Living God, you are the source of our strength;
All: **When uncertainty and weakness grip us,**
you will build us up.
One: Living God, you are the source of our faith;
All: **In Jesus Christ you have given us the Sign to believe in.**
One: Living God, you are the source of all our time;
All: **With us now, your love lasts through all eternity.**

Opening Prayer

One: Bring us together to worship, O God.
All: **Give us joy and renewal,**
as we offer praise and thanksgiving to you.
One: Bring us together to create community, O God.
All: **Give us fellowship and encouragement,**
as we seek to work together.
One: Bring us together to follow the Way of Jesus, O God.
All: **Give us inspiration and staying power,**
as we consider Christ's wisdom, and as we reflect on Christ's
concern for the poor and challenged.
One: Bring us together to serve those without power, O God.
All: **Give us gentle justice, and a willingness to work with those who**
are oppressed. Amen.

Prayer of Confessional Questions

One: There is a gap between your Way and our way, O God.

All: **Your Way stresses rich nations sharing with poor nations, but our way…?**

One: There is a gap between your Way, and our way, O God.

All: **Your Way involves a willingness to empower the downtrodden and rejected, but our way…?**

One: There is a gap between your Way, and our way, O God.

All: **Your Way works for peace where there is conflict and harsh words, but our way…?**

One: There is a gap between your Way and our way, O God.

All: **Your Way is sensitive to the needs and the feelings of others, but our way…?**

(Time for silent reflection)

Words of Assurance

One: Into our troubled hearts and minds you will breathe your peace, O God, but you require that we actively work with you to bring change.

All: **We will take the time to reflect on our attitudes,**
we will take the time to consider our lifestyle,
we will have the courage to make changes for simplicity,
we will work to bridge the gap between rich and poor,
we will not be discouraged!

One: God's peace will be your peace!

All: **God be praised! Amen.**

Offering Prayer

One: Bless these gifts, O God, for they are symbols of hope in a troubled world.

All: **Through them, the lonely will come into community,**
through them, your Word will be heard,
through them, children will joyfully come to faith,
through them, the sick will be visited,
through them, the bereaved will receive comfort,
through them, people far away will receive practical help,
through them, the poor will be supported,
through them, the Way of Jesus Christ will be followed.

One: You will bless these gifts, O God, and we will be the persons who work to make them effective gifts. Amen.

Commissioning

One: We go forth in the power of Jesus Christ,

All: A confronter of evil,
an example of empathy,
a person of justice,
a friend of children,
a noticer of widows,
a peace-bringer to the disturbed,
a community founder,
an influence of God's love.

One: Go forth in the power of Jesus Christ!
Ready to live each day fully,
ready to express yourself with confidence,
ready to renew ties of family of friendship,
ready to speak up for the poor.

All: Our loving God goes with us!

Sunday between
October 2 and 8 inclusive

Proper 22 [27]

(celebrated as Worldwide Communion)

Lamentations 1:1–6
Lamentations 3:19–26 or Psalm 137
2 Timothy 1:1–14
Luke 17:5–10

Call to Worship

One: We gather as members of *(name of church)* faith community; to pray, to praise, and to remember.

All: In bread and wine unite us, O God.

One: We gather in solidarity with Christians of every continent; Christians of many denominations.

All: In bread and wine unite us, O God.

One: We gather as disciples of Jesus Christ, to hear words of truth, compassion, and justice.

All: In bread and wine unite us, O God.

One: We gather in the tradition of the saints, to be strengthened and serve faithfully.

All: In bread and wine unite us, O God.

Opening Prayer

One: Loving God, we thank you for everything which joins us together as church:

**All: Our study of the Bible, our common meals and picnics,
our support of the powerless, our friendship and fellowship,
our sacraments of Baptism and Holy Communion;
our following of Jesus' Way.**

One: Loving God, we thank you for this faith community,
and for our membership in the wider church of Jesus Christ:

All: Our links with other city/town churches,
the joy we find in our own denomination,
and our contacts with the global church.
Through your Holy Spirit, O God,
bring us closer together in faith and work,
and inspire us with the hope "that all may be one." Amen.

Prayer of Confession

One: In moments of reflection, we pause as our prayer reaches out to touch persons we know and love, far from this city, in other states/provinces, and in other countries. We remember especially those with deep needs.
Hold in your thoughts specific persons.
(Time for silent reflection)

One: Loving God,
All: **May your love surround those for whom we pray.**
One: There is a distance between us and some others which cannot be measured in miles or kilometers; the distance caused by conflict, by harsh words uttered, by guilt, by envy, by feelings unexpressed. It troubles us.
Hold in your mind's eye, a specific person or persons.
(Time for silent reflection)

One: Loving God,
All: **Grant us the will to make the first move towards reconciliation.**
One: Our prayer reaches out to touch those Christian communities that we know and love; and also those communities embraced and supported by the wider church.
Picture a specific church or Christian cause.
(Time for silent reflection)

One: Loving God,

All: **Give us a broad and generous understanding of "the church."**

One: Where our commitment to the faith community has been half-hearted, where our concern for the wider church has been slight, open our minds to fresh choices.
Think of a new way of supporting the community of Jesus Christ.
(Time for silent reflection)

One: Loving God,

All: **Grant us the will to help, through prayer and action, the church beyond this faith community. Amen.**

Words of Assurance

All: **In recognition of the need to deepen our life of faith,
in renewed commitment to the whole faith community
of Jesus Christ,
in a willingness to speak boldly, and act courageously,
we will reach a new starting point.**

One: You will, and God's pardon and peace will be yours.

All: **Thanks be to God! Amen.**

Offering Prayer

One: In the bread broken, we recognize the broken nature of persons, relationships, and hopes, and the gifts we need to bring healing and wholeness.

All: **In the wine poured out, we recognize the sadness poured out through loss of loved ones, hope, and health, and the gifts we need to bring new life.**

One: In our money shared, we recognize the resources we have available to change our neighborhood, our church, and our world for good.

All: **Bless these and all our gifts given to us to do the work of Jesus Christ in this day and generation. Amen.**

Commissioning

One: Loving God, as we continue our Christian journey, give us faith:

All: Faith, as we face the challenges of home and work and school,
faith, as we pray and reflect and dream,
faith, as we find the confidence to try new endeavors,
faith, as we mend broken relationships,
faith, as we appreciate the faithfulness of other Christian traditions,
faith, as we work with other churches,
faith, as we realize that your love, O God, is with us
and will never let us go.

Sunday between
October 2 and 8 inclusive

Proper 22 [27]

Lamentations 1:1–6
Psalm 137
2 Timothy 1:1–14
Luke 17:5–10

Call to Worship

One: Mysterious God, creating cosmos, universe, and planet; joining atom to atom, molecule to molecule,

All: In the energy of life, we praise you!

One: Compassionate God, revealing your freeing presence to Moses, your justice to Amos, your parental love to Jesus,

All: In the lives of your faithful ones, we know you!

One: Faith-community God, gathering your people in hope, sustaining them in hardship, calling them in loving action,

All: Through the life of this fellowship, we serve you!

Prayer of Thanksgiving

One: We give you thanks, Living God,
for the world in which we live.

All: Encourage us to preserve the water, the air, and the wildlife of this finite planet.

One: We give you thanks, Living God, for our homes and families,

All: Encourage us to support the vulnerable, listen to the troubled, and share with those who have needs.

One: We give you thanks, Living God,
for this Christian community of which we are members.

All: Encourage us to worship joyfully, give generously, and work with others to reflect Jesus Christ, its founder and head. Amen.

Prayer of Confession

One: If Christ is for us, who can be against us?

All: **The market economy, the forces of getting and spending, will not win through.**

One: If Christ is for us, who can be against us?

All: **The dark place of depression, the apathy which keeps us uninvolved, will not defeat Christ.**

One: If Christ is for us, who can be against us?

All: **Our downplaying of abilities, our reluctance to get involved, will not shut Christ out.**

One: If Christ is for us, who can be against us?

All: **The devaluing of church, the low priority of worship for so many, will not overcome the relevance of Jesus, for our time.**

One: If Christ is with us who can be against us?

All: **The struggle with forces of evil and terror, the feelings of vulnerability, cannot withstand Christ.**

(Time for silent reflection)

Words of Assurance

One: Your attitude will be the one Christ Jesus possessed. He did not compromise with evil, but stood up to it. He stayed faithful to God, and took the hard road to the cross.

All: **We do not find it easy to keep Christian values to the fore, but we will try; we have the example of Jesus before us.**

One: Your faithfulness will bring you freedom and peace.

All: **Thanks be to God. Amen.**

Offering Prayer

One: This is the way we nourish our faith, and the faith of others: by giving simple gifts, and making sure they are well used.

All: **Our gifts will make the truth clear.**
   Our gifts will root out suspicion.
   Our gifts will attack small-mindedness.
   Our gifts will shout out "injustice."
   Our gifts will sit beside the suffering and comfort the dying.

One: Enabling God, bless our gifts of money, and combine time and talent with them, to increase their effectiveness.

All: **Amen.**

Commissioning

One: God goes with you as you leave the church, and God will go with you in the coming week.

All: **God's strength will get us through the rough patches,**
God's grace will sustain us when the world lets us down,
God's essential goodness will counter the corruption around us,
God's acceptance will model our response to prejudice,
God's love will embrace us and keep us eternally secure.

Sunday between
October 9 and 15 inclusive

Proper 23 [28]

Jeremiah 29:1, 4–7
Psalm 66:1–12
2 Timothy 2:8–15
Luke 17:11–19

Call to Worship *(adapted from Psalm 66)*

One: Praise God, with shouts of joy, all people.

All: Sing to the glory of God's name, offer the Holy One glorious praise.

One: Praise God, whose presence has been with the faithful ones in times past.

All: With the people of Israel when they escaped from Egypt, with the immigrants and refugees coming into the land of promise.

One: Praise God, whose care is for each person, struggling or free.

All: God hears our prayers, loves us, and gives us new life.

Opening Prayer

One: You call us, O God, to settle down as we worship you,

All: To rejoice in the routine of wholehearted praise.

One: You call us, O God, to settle down in our life of prayer,

All: To regularly bring our thanks and our deepest concerns before you, and to listen.

One: You call us, O God, to settle down in your service,

All: To find joy as we work within this faith community, and as self-serving values of our society are challenged.

One: You call us, O God, to settle down as we follow Jesus,

All: To ready ourselves for the opposition of the powerful, and to find fulfillment in the long haul of discipleship. Amen.

Prayer of Confession

One: You want us to be whole and healthy, Living God, healthy in body.

All: **You are with us as we watch our diet, and when we regularly exercise.**

One: You want us to be whole and healthy, Living God, healthy in mind.

All: **You are with us as we explore new ideas and theories, and when we discuss issues with our friends.**

One: You want us to be whole and healthy, Living God, emotionally healthy.

All: **You are with us as we share our feelings, and when we hear the deepest anxieties of others.**

One: You want us to be whole and healthy, Living God, healthy in spirit.

All: **You are with us as we explore the scriptures with openness, and when we share our faith life with others.**

(Time for silent reflection)

Words of Assurance

One: Health of body, mind, and spirit will not come without effort. It requires careful reflection and time.

All: **We are ready to put time and effort into searching out the sources of dis-ease in our beings, and making necessary changes.**

One: Pardon and peace will be yours.

All: **Thanks be to God! Amen.**

Offering Prayer

One: These are our gifts to promote wholeness and healing, O God.

All: **They will go to work in community center and hospital.**
They will go to work in the homes of this faith community.
They will go to work in our home.
And in places far from here, among those whose names we will never know.
These gifts will be effective.

One: Bless them, as we dedicate ourselves to the healing, reconciling work of Jesus Christ. Amen.

Commissioning

One: You come to us in a healing moment, O God.

All: **You give us hope, when the darkness seems overwhelming.**

You give us courage, when we want to run and hide.

You give us the will to break out, when we feel in a rut.

You give us the warmth of friendship, when our aloneness chills us.

You go with us now, our companion and our guide.

Sunday between
October 16 and 22 inclusive

Proper 24 [29]

(Celebrated as Peace Sabbath)

Jeremiah 31:27–34
Psalm 119:97–104
2 Timothy 3:14 – 4:5
Luke 18:1–8

Call to Worship

One: What you have promised, you have given, O God!

All: **You have given us a good world, and the means of keeping it good.**

One: What you have promised, you have given, O God!

All: **You have given us your Word, and the means of interpreting it, for our day and age.**

One: What you have promised, you have given, O God!

All: **You have given your Covenant, you will never leave us or let us down.**

One: What you have promised, you have given, O God!

All: **You have shown us your Way in Jesus Christ, and given us the will to follow faithfully.**

Opening Prayer

One: You have graced us with this hour of peace, O God.

All: **We give you thanks and praise, and know that you are with us.**

One: You have graced us with this hour of peace, O God.

All: **We reflect and confess, and know that you will pardon us.**

One: You have graced us with this hour of peace, O God.

All: **We are challenged to strengthen this faith community, and we know that you will work with us.**

One: You have graced us with this hour of peace, O God.

All: **We are people in an unjust, conflict-ridden and polluted world, and we know that you will enable us to bring change.**

One: You have graced us with this hour of peace, O God.

**All: We have been touched by Jesus the peace-bringer,
and we know that he will inspire us. Amen.**

Or

Opening Prayer

One: We ask for the gift of persistence, O God,

All: When we believe in the rightness and integrity of the cause.

One: We ask for the gift of persistence, O God,

**All: To carry on even when the doubters and mockers make their
presence felt.**

One: We ask for the gift of persistence, O God,

All: To counter low self-esteem and strong opposition.

One: We ask for the gift of persistence, O God,

**All: A persistence applauded by Jesus,
a persistence in opposing the evil ones,
a persistence that his life's pattern showed so clearly. Amen.**

Prayer of Confession

One: Create peace within us, O God.

**All: When emotions swirl, when memories haunt,
when decisions do not come easily,
be our source of peace, O God.**

One: Create peace around us, O God.

**All: When indifference rules, when friends surprise,
when situations test us,
be our source of peace, O God.**

One: Create peace through us, O God.

**All: When injustice is clear, when a word needs speaking,
when action is called for,
be our will for peace, O God.**

One: Create peace in our faith community, O God.

**All: When we need to support each other,
when we serve the wider church,**

when we face the hurts of a suffering world,
be our inspiration for peace, O God.
> *(Time for silent reflection)*

Words of Assurance

One: Peace does not come effortlessly. It requires openness to new insights, death to old hostilities, and the willingness to accept a new way.

All: **We are ready to take up the challenge and accept a new vision.**

One: Peace is God's graceful gift to you.

All: **Thanks be to God! Amen.**

Offering Prayer

One: Through these gifts, the cause of peace will go forward:

All: **Peace for the troubled heart and mind,**
peace within the communities of faith,
peace where conflict rages,
peace where evil infiltrates,
peace where silence deadens,
peace where listening renews.

One: The peace of Jesus Christ; the peace that he taught, the peace that he died for.

All: **Bless, O God, these offerings and all our gifts, and work joyfully with them. Amen.**

Commissioning

One: Be peacemakers!

All: **Where there is trouble and anxiety we will bring calm.**

One: Be peace restorers!

All: **Where persons are at odds with one another, we will bring reconciliation.**

One: Be examples of peacefulness!

All: **In the midst of the hustle and hurry of this world, we will take time to smell the roses.**

One: Be God's peaceful people!

All: **We will find peace in prayer, and fulfillment in working for peace.**

Sunday between
October 23 and 29 inclusive

Proper 25 [30]

Joel 2:23–32
Psalm 65
2 Timothy 4:6–8, 16–18
Luke 18:9–14

Call to Worship

One: Creator of calm,

All: Even with our uneasiness and fear, we approach you.

One: Promise of forgiveness,

All: Even though we are aware of our shortcomings, we approach you.

One: Giver of hope,

All: Even though we lack confidence for the journey, we approach you.

One: Source of compassion,

All: Even though we lack your healing spirit, we approach you.

Opening Prayer

One: More than having great wealth,

All: We appreciate your wonderful creation, O God.

One: More than fame and popularity,

All: We value the pattern of Jesus Christ, O God.

One: More than belonging to an exclusive group,

All: We are glad to be members of your faith community, O God.

One: More than anything else in all the world,

All: We rejoice in your gracious love for us, O God. Amen.

Prayer of Confession

One: Loving God, when we see ourselves as a cut above others,

All: Bring us down to earth.

One: Loving God, when we insist on our own way,

All: Enable us to understand what that means, to those close to us.

One: Loving God, when we ignore the crying needs around us,

All: Wake us up to respond to them.

One: Loving God, when we are full of our own self-importance,

All: Put a child in our midst.

One: Loving God, when we trumpet our own greatness,

All: Show us the path that leads to humility.

(Time for silent reflection)

Words of Assurance

One: O God, you will not let us get above ourselves.

You encourage us to reflect on our lifestyle and attitudes,

in the light of Jesus Christ, who walked humbly to the cross.

All: The simple way of Jesus is before us; we will follow him faithfully.

One: God's pardon and peace will be yours.

All: Thanks be to God. Amen.

Offering Prayer

One: Gifts without measure, you have given to us, O God.

All: We rejoice that we are able to return gifts for your work.

One: May these our gifts be humbly shared,

All: With the distressed, as they come to know peace;
with the bereaved, as they sense a comforting presence;
with the powerless, as they find a way to be in control;
with the challenged, as their special gifts are affirmed.

One: As these gifts go to work, your presence is felt!

All: Thanks be to you, O God! Amen.

Commissioning

One: The listening is over, now is the time for action!

All: We will have done with self-glorification,
we will have done with self-justification,
we will have done with denial,
we will have done with apathy,
we will have done with pride.

One: And you will walk humbly before your God?

All: We will!

Sunday between
October 30 and November 5 inclusive

Proper 26 [31]

(not celebrated as All Saints' Day)

Habakkuk 1:1–4, 2:1–4
Psalm 119:137–144
2 Thessalonians 1:1–4, 11–12
Luke 19:1–10

Call to Worship

One: Wonderful Covenant Maker, we come before you.

All: **We are your people and you are our God, and we rejoice!**

One: Great Teacher from the beginning, we come before you.

All: **We are ready for fresh understanding; your Word will open up new ideas.**

One: Source of all Forgiveness, we come before you.

All: **Our sins and shortcomings trouble us; we are ready to begin again.**

One: Eternal Loved One, we come before you.

All: **We know that your love at the depth of our being,
your love at the heart of our church, will transform everything.**

Opening Prayer

One: Loving God, you have come close to us in Jesus Christ.
You know the whole range of human experience.
In times of joy and celebration, Loving God,

All: **You laugh with us, you affirm our self-worth,
you strengthen us as family and community.**

One: In times of uncertainty and change, Loving God,

All: **You are the Rooted One. You hold us fast when the storm strikes home.**

One: In times of loss, when our most cherished dreams have been taken away from us, Loving God,

All: **You are the Enduring One, the promise of deep peace. Amen.**

Or

Opening Prayer

One: Loving God, we have heard so much about Jesus. We want to see him more clearly.

All: **We are a part of the faithful group who wait with enthusiasm for Jesus to be present.**

One: We want his message to come home to us. We are ready to take it to heart.

All: **The message touches deep feelings and prepares us for difficult choices.**

One: The changes that we will make will open up a new way of life for us,

All: **The past will be put in the past; a faithful future beckons.**

One: It is hard to believe the difference the Way of Jesus will make,

All: **Yet we are determined to go that way, and dance and sing as we go! Amen.**

Prayer of Confession

One: Sometimes we have lost our way, O God.

All: **We know the right course of action, but lack the courage to follow it.**

One: Sometimes we have missed our cue, O God.

All: **We are aware of what needs to be said, but are afraid of the consequences.**

One: Sometimes we have labeled others unfairly, O God.

All: **We are quick to judge on the basis of race or speech, slow to accept the worth of the person.**

One: Sometimes we have avoided the challenge, O God.

All: **The call to justice or to compassion comes clearly to us, but we let it pass.**

One: Sometimes we have been unfaithful, O God.

All: **The example of Jesus Christ is before us, but we deny our discipleship.**

   (Time for silent reflection)

Words of Assurance

One: Jesus said to the reformed tax collector Zacchaeus, "Today salvation has come to this house."

All: We rejoice that we can confess our shortcomings fully and openly, and can make a fresh start, as he did.

One: God's pardon and peace are yours.

All: Thanks be to God! Amen.

Offering Prayer

One: In our giving, O God, the life of Jesus is before us.

All: We will give to maintain Christ's values,
we will give to sustain Christ's work,
we will give to show Christ's compassion,
we will give to strengthen Christ's community,
we will give because we remember Christ's cross,
and experience his risen hope.

One: And you, O God, will receive our gifts, and bless them.

All: Amen.

Commissioning

One: Go the extra mile!

All: We will go out of the way to strengthen our faith.

One: Stay the course!

All: We will endure with the person to whom trouble has come.

One: Forgive generously!

All: We will put hard feelings aside, and restore the ties of friendship.

One: Live fully!

All: We will rejoice in each day's opportunities, and make the most of them.

Sunday between
November 6 and 12 inclusive

Proper 27 [32]

Haggai 1:15b – 2:9
Psalm 145:1–5, 17–21 or Psalm 98
2 Thessalonians 2:1–5, 13–17
Luke 20:27–38

Call to Worship *(based on Psalm 145)*

One: We will proclaim your greatness as we worship, O Loving God.

All: **We will proclaim your greatness. From generation to generation, you have inspired your people.**

One: We will proclaim your mercy as we worship, O Loving God.

All: **We will proclaim your mercy. Through deeds of compassion and sacrifice, your Way has been made known.**

One: We will proclaim your justice as we worship, O Loving God.

All: **We will proclaim your justice. Your people have fed the hungry and encouraged the powerless.**

One: We will proclaim your faithfulness as we worship, O Loving God.

All: **We will proclaim your faithfulness. Those who suffer loss and live in fear have known your sustaining presence.**

Opening Prayer

One: How can we worship worthily, O most worthy God?

All: **You open our hearts, giving wing to our voices, and you touch the depths of our spirits.**

One: How can we work together in the faith community, O God of the Church?

All: **You encourage us to commitment, you give us community/friendship as we eat and laugh together.**

One: How can we broaden our horizons, universal God?

All: **You set the needs of our neighborhood and our troubled world clearly before us; you set us to work.**

One: How can we witness to the significance of Jesus, O most loving God?

All: **You give us the disciple model, a willingness to listen to inspired teaching, a willingness to practice an unselfish way, a willingness to leave behind the tried and proven path.**

One: May the God whom we praise, the God who gathers us together, the God known in Jesus, hear our prayer.

All: **Amen.**

Prayer of Confession

One: You ask us the hard questions, O God.

All: **You ask, can we come to forgive wholeheartedly those who have hurt us deeply?**

One: You ask us the hard questions, O God.

All: **You ask, can we face the reality of broken relationships and ambitions that cannot be realized?**

One: You ask us the hard questions, O God.

All: **You ask, can we let go the habits which hold us bound, the attitudes which betray our prejudice?**

One: You ask us the hard questions, O God.

All: **You ask, can we see the poverty and exploitation of women and children in the developing world, and remain unmoved?**

(Time for silent reflection)

Words of Assurance

One: In Jesus Christ, you have shown us the range of hard questions that can be asked.

In Jesus Christ, you have given us examples of how hard questions can be faced.

In Jesus Christ, you have shown us that apathy and fear can be overcome.

All: **As we follow Christ, we know our hard questions can be answered.**

One: Pardon and peace is for you!

All: **Thanks be to God! Amen.**

Offering Prayer

One: To you, O God, we joyfully present our gifts.

All: **Through them, faith will counter unbelief,**
hope will counter despair,
fellowship will counter loneliness,
and mission will counter self-serving.

One: Bless these gifts, O God, for action in the Spirit of Jesus Christ.

All: **Amen.**

Commissioning

One: Number us among your faithful people, O God,

All: **Ready for the roller-coaster ride of learning,**
prepared to relentlessly question "the way it has always been done,"
never satisfied if people are suffering and authorities are complacent,
ready to build community as a base for venturing out,
looking always to Jesus, who took nothing for granted.

Sunday between
November 13 and 19 inclusive

Proper 28 [33]

Isaiah 65:17–25
Isaiah 12
2 Thessalonians 3:6–13
Luke 21:5–19

Call to Worship

One: God spoke to Abraham.

All: Abraham heard God's voice, and set out confidently into the unknown.

One: God challenged Moses.

All: Moses heard God's voice, and brought freedom to a people.

One: God empowered Amos.

All: Amos heard God's voice, and exposed attitudes of selfishness and greed to the light of day.

One: God anointed Jesus.

All: Jesus was aware of God's presence, and lives to transform human-kind.

One: God's call comes to our faith community.

All: We respond to God's call with worship and with life-bringing work.

Opening Prayer

One: We seek to come into loving relationship with you, our Living God. As a parent holds in close embrace a child who is cherished and loved,

All: So we are aware of your compassion to us, most caring God.

One: As a grandparent models patience and generosity to a grandchild,

All: So we are aware of your graciousness to us and to all humankind, most giving God.

One: As a best friend is able to listen to the deepest longings of heart and soul,

All: **So we are aware of your heartfelt concern for us, O ever-present God.**

One: Deepen our relationship with you, Loving God, that created in your image and empowered by the example of Jesus Christ,

we may be enabled to change our small corner of the world, for good.

All: **Amen.**

Prayer of Confession

One: Stand firm! Be ready for subtle tests and temptations.

All: **We will "look before we leap," and think carefully before we speak.**

One: Prepare thoroughly! Plan carefully for faithful ventures.

All: **We will take the preparation time we need,**
before committing ourselves to the tasks of Christ.

One: Be on your guard! Respond promptly to the call to stand with the vulnerable and powerless.

All: **We will not turn down the call to compassionate action, just**
because it interferes with our personal plans.

One: Dedicate yourselves to the Way of Christ! Heart, mind, and spirit need to be engaged, if the Way is to be followed faithfully.

All: **We will give priority to our Christian responsibilities,**
but we will not neglect our family and friends.

One: Be alert! Stand ready for the act of terror, the revenge of fanatical men and women.

All: **If our faith in God is sure, if our spirits are prayerfully alive, then**
nothing will overcome us.

(Time for silent reflection)

Words of Assurance

One: Your careful reflection, and your determination to act, will identify you as a faithful disciple.

All: **We will not shrink from the tough journey,**
and we will have fun as we do Christ's work.

One: God's peace will be your peace.

All: **Thanks be to God! Amen.**

Offering Prayer

One: Receive our gifts, Loving God, and with them receive the firm intention, of this faith community,

All: **To praise joyfully,**
to create opportunities,
to renew self-confidence,
to encourage fresh starts,
to comfort the sick and bereaved,
to nurture the disheartened,
to encourage faithfulness,
to practice mission,
in the Way of Jesus. Amen.

Commissioning

One: We are ready for God's work in the coming week.

All: **We will listen carefully,**
we will prepare thoroughly,
we will encourage with sensitivity,
we will vision faithfully,
we will work creatively,
we will care compassionately,
we will speak out boldly,
we will follow Christ joyfully.

One: And God will go with you!

Last Sunday before Advent

Reign of Christ Sunday

Jeremiah 23:1–6
Luke 1:68–79 or Psalm 46
Colossians 1:11–20
Luke 23:33–43

Call to Worship

One: Christ reigns!

All: **Christ reigns to open our hearts with thanksgiving.**

One: Christ reigns!

All: **Christ reigns to bring us together in fellowship.**

One: Christ reigns!

All: **Christ reigns to deepen our prayers and enliven our praise.**

One: Christ reigns!

All: **Christ reigns to put our faith into practice.**
Reign over our hearts and minds and actions, Christ Jesus.

Opening Prayer

One: We seek your rule over us, O Christ!

All: **You call us to believe in ourselves, and in our unique talents and abilities.**

One: We are ready for your guidance, O Christ!

All: **Your words in scripture, and the actions of faithful saints, show us the way.**

One: We know your leading presence in our church, O Christ!

All: **You call us to be open to new truth, and to support our sisters and brothers in the faith.**

One: We seek your rule over us, O Christ!

All: **Many powers call on us to submit and follow. You alone hold before us the power of God's love. Amen.**

Prayer of Confession

One: We confess, Living God, those powers to which we submit.
We submit to the power of self-focus, self-concern.
Our own needs and anxieties hold us bound.

All: **We will be freed to leave behind the domination of self.**
We will work to break from the ties which bind us.

One: We submit to the power of despair.
We look at the needs of our community, our conflict-ridden world, and our polluted environment, and we say, "What difference can one person make?"

All: **We will be freed to deepen our understanding of the issues and get involved for change.**

One: We submit to the power of apathy.
We know action is required to restore relationships, to establish friendship, and to break the cycle of injustice and poverty, but we hang back.

All: **We will be freed to take the necessary steps, and to make a faithful move for good.**

(Time for silent reflection)

Words of Assurance

One: O God, no binding power is beyond your will to free.

All: **As we recognize those powers which hold us in their grip,**
as we confront and struggle with those powers,
as we overcome them with your faithful assistance,
new ways open up; new life is ours!

One: The restrictions of the past are broken; the peace of God is yours.

All: **Thanks be to God. Amen.**

Offering Prayer

One: Transform our gifts, O God!

All: **May they preach the good news.**
May they comfort the distressed.
May they stand beside the bereaved.
May they provide water in the desert, and light in the dark places.

One: Transform our gifts, O God, and bless those who bring them to life.

All: **Amen.**

Commissioning

One: Go from this place to proclaim the Rule of Christ!

All: **In the midst of self-serving, we will proclaim generosity;**
in the midst of prejudice, we will proclaim acceptance;
in the midst of loss, we will proclaim a ray of hope;
in the midst of tangled values, we will proclaim the Living Word.

One: Go into the world, to proclaim the Rule of Christ!

All: **Where abuse goes unchecked, we will proclaim action;**
where suffering is found, we will proclaim a healing peace;
where sin and guilt drag people down, we will proclaim forgiveness;
where wealth and privilege meet poverty and powerlessness;
we will proclaim justice and fair sharing.

All Saints' Day

(November 1, or 1st Sunday in November)

Daniel 7:1–3, 15–18
Psalm 149
Ephesians 1:11–23
Luke 6:20–31

Call to Worship

One: The saints invite us to worship God.

All: Saint Francis calls us to assess our needs and priorities.

One: The saints invite us to come into God's presence.

All: Saint Patrick calls us to combat the worship of popular gods.

One: The saints invite us to realize the justice of our God.

All: Dietrich Bonhoeffer calls us to determine the extent of our commitment.

One: The saints invite us to see the compassion of our God.

All: Oscar Romero calls us to face the people of power, without fear.

Opening Prayer

One: In the first mists of creation,

All: You were there, O God.

One: When Abraham and Sarah knew you, and responded to your call,

All: You were strength in the unknown for them, O God.

One: In the inspiring, yet challenging words of Jeremiah and Amos,

All: You pointed the way to truth and justice, O God.

One: As Jesus recognized you as his loving parent,
and made your Way his Way,

All: Your inspiration brought him joy, and the hard road which led to a cross.

One: When modern saints and prophets, like Martin Luther King and
Mother Teresa, faithfully followed Jesus,

All: Your Spirit touched them, and through them brought courage, healing, and comfort.

One: And you are with us, O Loving God,

All: And will be eternally. Amen.

Prayer of Confession

One: A mark of sainthood is loving God with all our heart, and all our mind, and all our strength.

All: Our love has wavered, our commitment has been lukewarm.

One: A mark of sainthood is loving ourselves.

All: We have questioned our self-confidence, devalued our gifts and skills, discounted our venturing courage.

One: A mark of sainthood is loving our neighbor as we love ourselves.

All: We have hung back from helping the poor, the hungry, and those who mourn.
We have chosen to ignore the distant ones, and written off the untrustworthy ones.

(Time for silent reflection)

Words of Assurance

One: We who have been marked at baptism with the Cross of Jesus Christ, will discover our sainthood,

All: As we gain confidence in the God who loves us,
as our self-confidence is restored and affirmed,
as we encourage each other within the faith community,
as we meet the needs of the hungry, the poor, and those who have suffered loss.

One: With renewal comes God's peace.

All: Thanks be to God! Amen.

Offering Prayer

One: Inspired by the commitment of saints in times past;
rejoicing in our present opportunity to support this faith community;

All: Giving through our mission funds, so that the saints at home and abroad will know solid support in coming months;

One: We ask your blessing on these gifts, O God.

All: We have put our money where our faith is, and we give thanks.
Amen.

Commissioning

One: The saints of all the ages go with us:

All: **Calling us to commitment,**
preparing us for struggle,
binding us into community,
readying us for learning,
steeling us for hardship,
reminding us of Jesus Christ and his Cross.

One: In their company we have nothing to fear!

All: **We have not, God be praised!**

Or

Commissioning

One: Remember the faithfulness of those who have served in past days.

All: **We remember, and we look to match their enthusiasm.**

One: Remember the courage of those who have served in past days.

All: **We remember, and we will be steadfast in the struggle.**

One: Remember the willingness to risk, of those who served in past days.

All: **We remember, and we will not be satisfied with blindly accepting**
tradition.

One: Remember the discipleship of those who have faithfully followed.

All: **We remember; we too are disciples of Jesus Christ.**

Thanksgiving

(4th Thursday in November, U.S.; 2nd Monday in October, Canada)

Deuteronomy 26:1–11
Psalm 100
Philippians 4:4–9
John 6:25–35

Call to Worship

One: Worship God with thanksgiving!

All: God gives us joyful songs to sing.

One: Worship God with thanksgiving!

All: God made us; we belong to God. We are the people of God, members of the faith community.

One: Worship God with thanksgiving!

All: We will serve God without holding back, for God is good. God's fulfillment lasts forever.

One: Worship God with thanksgiving!

All: God's Chosen One Jesus feeds mind and spirit; Jesus is the bread of life.

Prayer of Thanksgiving

One: Wonderful are your gifts, O God:
golden leaves, refreshing rain, the grandeur of the mountains.

All: Wonderful are your gifts, O God; joyful is our thanksgiving.

One: Loved ones are your gifts, O God:
friends who can be relied on, caring mothers and fathers, happy children and grandchildren.

All: Loved ones are your gifts, O God; heartfelt is our thanksgiving.

One: The church is your gift, O God:
worshipping with enthusiasm, growing in fellowship, serving the powerless.

All: The church is your gift, O God; faith-filled is our thanksgiving.

One: Jesus is your gift, O God:
working with the challenged ones, defeating evil on the cross, gloriously risen.

All: Jesus is your gift, O God; endless is our thanksgiving. Amen.

Prayer of Confession

One: Our thanksgiving rises to you, O God, on the wings of song and the
        joy of dance.

All: **When we are fearful of giving expression to our thanks, forgive us!**

One: Our thanksgiving finds expression, O God, when the disadvantaged are
        identified and the lowly ones affirmed.

All: **When we are apathetic about encouraging the downhearted and
        supporting the weak, forgive us!**

One: Our thanksgiving comes home to us, O God, when our way of life, our
        health, or our chance of fulfillment takes a turn for the better.

All: **When we are without hope of change, when we will not see the
        light, forgive us!**

One: Our thanksgiving breaks barriers, O God, breaks through the
        limitations of nation, race, and status.

All: **When we keep ourselves to ourselves, when fear or apathy prevents
        us from taking risks, forgive us!**

One: Our thanksgiving finds a focus, O God, in the person of Jesus Christ.

All: **When we fail to see his image in the crucified ones today, when we
        hang back from following his way, forgive us!**
        (Time for silent reflection)

Words of Assurance

One: Thanksgiving calls us to repentance, O God.

All: **Thanksgiving becomes a reality,
        as old challenges are squarely faced,
        as new insights are taken to heart,
        as we find fresh courage to go in a faithful direction.**

One: God's peace will be your peace from this moment on.

All: **Thanks be to God! Amen.**

Offering Prayer

One: Loving God, our eyes sparkle with thanksgiving for the beauty that
        surrounds us.

All: **Our voices resound with thanksgiving for friends and family who are well-loved by us.**

One: Our living proclaims with enthusiasm the way Christ has made clear to us.

All: **Our giving is a joyful response to you, our abundantly gracious God. We will not keep it "in the family," but will reach out with our offerings of thanks to touch the needy ones of our world for good. Amen.**

Or

Offering Prayer

One: Bread. Grain, sown and harvested, milled and baked, crusty rolls, wholesome loaves.

All: **We thank you, God, source of creation, for your gifts of food.**

One: Bread of life. Hope to the sick, friend of the despised, proclaimer of God's Realm.

All: **We thank you, God, for Jesus, our inspiration and savior.**

One: Bread shared in faith community. Symbol of common faith life, spiritual food, nourishment for the faithful life.

All: **We thank you, God, for bread, shared with wine; the Communion which unites us; and the sign of the cross-love which astounds us.**

One: We have been blessed with bread, and with all the change for good these gifts make possible.

All: **Receive our heartfelt thanksgiving, wonderful God. Amen.**

Commissioning

One: Thanksgiving to you, O God.

All: **Thanksgiving for a glorious Creator,
thanksgiving for a community that sustains us,
thanksgiving for a word to challenge us,
thanksgiving for Jesus, the Way for us,
thanksgiving for your eternal Hope!**

One: O loving, joyful, and careful God,

All: **Thank you!**

Memorial/Remembrance/Veterans Sunday

Call to Worship

One: Past struggles shape us, O God.

All: We are called to remember their impact.

One: The heroism of ordinary men and women challenges us, O God.

All: We are called to honor their memory.

One: The dark side of conflict influences us, O God.

All: We are called to recognize its power.

One: The sacrifice of military personnel and civilians, humbles us, O God.

All: Greater love has no one than this, that one lays down one's life for another.

Opening Prayer *(for Memorial/Remembrance Day)*

One: Giving without counting the cost –

All: We come before you, O God, remembering those who gave up freedom, livelihood, even life, for their country and for their friends.

One: Fighting for a just cause –

All: We come before you, O God, alert to the needs of a hurting world, aware of our choices to bring healing.

One: Prepared to resist evil –

All: We come before you, O God, knowing the darkness of greed, apathy and self-interest, yet confident in the power of your loving light.

One: Ready for sacrifice –

All: We come before you, O God, seeing the Cross of Jesus before us, yet encouraged by that cross to make our discipleship effective and sustained. Amen.

Prayer of Confession: A Prayer for Peace

One: Create peace within us, O God.

All: When emotions swirl, when memories haunt, and decisions will not come easily; be our source of peace, O God.

One: Create peace around us, O God.

All: When indifference rules, when friends surprise, and situations test us; be our source of peace, O God.

One: Create peace through us, O God.

All: When injustice is clear, when a word needs speaking, when action is called for; be our will for peace, O God.

One: Create peace with our faith community, O God.

All: When we need to support each other, when we serve the wider church, when we face the hurts of a suffering world; be our inspiration for peace, O God.

    (Time for silent reflection)

Words of Assurance

One: Peace does not come effortlessly. It requires an openness to new insights, death to old hostilities, and the willingness to accept a new way.

All: We are ready to take up the challenge and accept a new vision.

One: Peace is God's graceful gift to you.

All: Thanks be to God. Amen.

Offering Prayer

One: Our gifts are tokens of our intentions:

All: to remember war's horror
    to bring peace,
    to end conflict,
    to counter suffering,
    to raise hopes,
    to bring new life.

One: Bless our gifts, O God, for they reflect the Sacrificed One, Jesus, who gave his life on a cross. Amen.

Or

Offering Prayer

One: We who give, remember those who gave all that they were, and all they had.

All: **Bless us in our giving.**
Use our gifts, that in their sharing, peace may become a reality.
We pray through the Prince of Peace. Amen.

Commissioning

One: Remember the sacrifice, and pray for an end to war.

All: **We remember, and we will strive to foster peace.**

One: Remember the suffering, and pray that enemies will be reconciled.

All: **We remember, and we will help to bring antagonists together.**

One: Remember the disturbed lives and terrorized persons.

All: **We remember, and we will give, to bring calm and security.**

One: Remember the hatred, and pray that love will replace it.

All: **We remember, and we will banish the hate that holds us bound.**

Thematic Index

Hebrew Scripture Index

New Testament Scripture Index

Also by David Sparks

Prayers to Share – Year B
Responsive Prayers for Each Sunday of the Church Year
Offers church leaders an entire year's worth of responsive prayers.
ISBN 1-55145-479-3

If you enjoyed this book you may also enjoy these other books from Wood Lake Books.

Living the Christ Life
Rediscovering the Seasons of the Christian Year
LOUISE MANGAN AND NANCY WYSE WITH LORI FARR
This valuable program resource for clergy, worship planners, and lay leaders offers practical tools for celebrating the Christian year at church and at home.
ISBN 1-55145-498-X

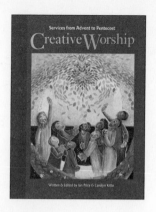

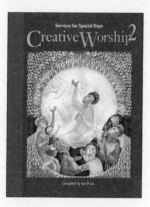

Creative Worship

Services from Advent to Pentecost
IAN PRICE & CAROLYN KITTO
Readings, songs, and other ideas to
build creative worship services for
all the major seasons of the Christian year. Includes a disk with a
complete text of the book.
ISBN 1-55145-461-0

Creative Worship 2

Services for Special Days
IAN PRICE
A compilation of worship services
from across Canada, Ausutralia, and
the USA. Includes an Earth Day
Service, A Service of Reconciliation
for Congregations in Conflict, and a
Service of Naming and Thanksgiving.
ISBN 1-55145-487-4

Youth Spirit

Program Ideas for Church Groups
Includes games, learning exercises,
integration activities, reflection
questions, worship suggestions, and
explanations of the church seasons.
ISBN 1-55145-247-2

Youth Spirit 2

More Program Ideas for Youth Groups
CHERYL PERRY
A multitude of flexible ideas to
create unique programs for youth
aged 12–18.
ISBN 1-55145-500-5

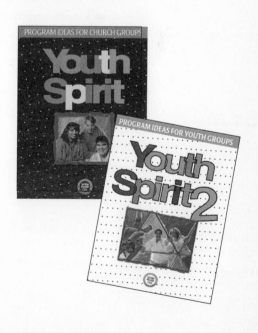

A Sensual Faith

Experiencing God Through Our Senses
IAN PRICE
A five-session, group study program
that explores each of the five senses
as a doorway to deepening our faith
and encountering God.
ISBN 1-55145-502-1

Spirit of Life

Five Studies to Bring Us Closer to God
IAN PRICE
Experience personal spiritual growth
through group study. Prayers and
daily reflections thread the five
sessions together.
ISBN 1-55145-432-7

Find these titles at any fine bookstore,
or call 1.800.663.2775 for more information.
Check our website www.joinhands.com